C000135060

101 CRAFT AND WORLD WHISKIES
TO TRY BEFORE YOU DIE

FULLY REVISED · 2ND EDITION · AND UPDATED

101 CRAFT AND WORLD WHISKIES
TO TRY BEFORE YOU DIE

IAN BUXTON

HEADLINE

First published in 2012 by HACHETTE SCOTLAND. Revised, updated and amended edition published in 2021 by HEADLINE PUBLISHING GROUP LTD.

1

Cataloguing in Publication Data is available from the British Library.

978 1 4722 7901 9

Designed by Lynn Carr

Printed and bound in Italy by L.E.G.O. S.p.A

All trademarks are acknowledged and all product images are copyright of the relevant brand owners, reproduced with permission.

Incidental imagery courtesy of Peter Bignell (page 6), Koval Distillery (page 11), Anssi Pysing (page 16), Reisetbauer Qualitätsbrand GmbH (page 220), Ian Buxton (pages 222–3), Martin Orozco/Lila Serenelli (page 224).

Hachette's policy is to use papers that are natural, renewable and recyclable products and made from wood grown in sustainable forests. The logging and manufacturing processes are expected to conform to the environmental regulations of the country of origin.

HEADLINE PUBLISHING GROUP

An Hachette UK Company Carmelite House
50 Victoria Embankment
London EC4Y 0DZ

www.headline.co.uk
www.hachette.co.uk

Contents

The spirit run at Belgrove, Tasmania, Australia.

Introduction

101 Craft and World Whiskies: what's that about?

Well, as far as 'world' whiskies go it's straightforward. It's generally agreed that there are five major whisky-producing nations: Canada, Ireland, Japan, Scotland and the USA; anywhere not on that list is a 'world' whisky producer. Note that I've listed them here, their first appearance in the book, in alphabetical order to avoid controversy.

But, controversially (that didn't last long, did it), if you were reading this in India you might point out – as from time to time the Indian government and their major distilling companies are prone to do – that India makes more 'whisky' than any of those five. In fact, India makes roughly the same quantity of spirit as all of them added together (more than 120 million cases, since you asked) but the vast majority of it, even the 'premium' stuff, is classified outside India as rum* and can't be sold as whisky. At least, not as we know it. Except for the Indian whisky that is actually whisky, which we'll discuss later.

So getting back to 'world' whisky, for the purposes of this book that covers anywhere not in the Big Five. Hence we have whisky here from Argentina, Australia, Austria, Belgium, Canada, Denmark, England, Finland, France, Germany, Iceland, India, Israel, Italy, Mexico, The Netherlands, New Zealand, South Africa, Spain, Sweden, Switzerland, Taiwan and Wales. We've included a fascinating selection of images of still houses, illustrating some different approaches to making whisky from round the world.

OK, that's the 'world' part. What about 'craft', because, as the more observant reader will have noticed, the 101 whiskies listed here also include examples from distilleries in Canada, Ireland and so on. Here's where definitions become more problematic because craft whisky is rather like pornography: hard to define but we know it when we see it.

Or do we, because one man's pornography is another's erotic art so, like the smutty pictures of old, the very term 'craft' is controversial and there's no one agreed definition of what it means. There's an implication of superior quality to it, not least because it generally appears alongside feel-good, clichéd epithets from the PR industry's word generator machine such as 'hand-crafted', 'artisanal', 'small batch' and *passionate*. Leaving aside the fact that it's just lazy writing, the key point about the p-word, which the PR industry appears to miss, is that it's incestuous and

---

* That's because it is. Often, well what shall we say, somewhat robust in style.

self-referential, so let's hope this is the only time this hackneyed term sullies these pages. It's about the producer, not the drinker – tell me what's in this drink for me, not for the people who made it.

Oh, and 'craft' whiskies and their makers have generally been on a 'journey', though where to, how we know they got there and why we should even pretend to care is frequently far from clear. Perhaps they simply travel in hope.

Faced with the growing use of this descriptor, a number of very large Scotch brands, blends and single malts got rather upset and were at pains to point out that a lot of 'craft', not to mention p*ss**n, went into the making of their whiskies. 'Craft' they were happy to imply was little more than a synonym for 'small' (though self-styled craft distillers generally prefer the term 'boutique') and small wasn't necessarily a guarantee of beauty – or quality, or great taste, or anything else for that matter. Other than being small, obviously.

Problem is, though, a lot of very large brands selling huge quantities of whisky would claim with some justice to have most if not all of the qualities which craft was appropriating.

And somewhere in every big brand's history we find a founder and a journey. Johnnie Walker, for example, which just happens to be the bestselling Scotch whisky in the world, was founded over 200 years ago by a real person – who, not entirely coincidentally, was called John Walker. If you asked anyone in the whisky business they would tell you that plenty of craftsmanship goes into the Walker blends and, as for authenticity, provenance and so on well, partly as Walker's pushback against craft claims, they had a PR guy toiling full-time for several years to produce a rather pompous book about the brand's long history.

The debate also ran hot and furious on social media, as such things are wont to do, and eventually a sort of consensus emerged. In the USA, people converged around the definition offered by the American Distilling Institute (ADI – the self-styled 'voice of craft distilling') who offer this guidance of a 'craft-distilled spirit': 'The products of an -independently -owned distillery with maximum annual sales of 100,000 proof gallons where the product is PHYSICALLY [their capitals] distilled and bottled on site.'

Just to be clear, that's a US definition, where a 'proof gallon' means 'one liquid gallon of spirits that is 50 per cent alcohol at 60 degrees F'. But, as every British tourist who's filled a rental at an American gas station knows, a regular US gallon is smaller than the UK version. They were the same until 1824 when the UK standardised a number of weights and measures, but the USA has clung on to the old Queen Anne gallon ever since – the imperial gallon is about 20 per cent larger at 4.55 litres, compared to 3.785 litres. Incidentally, they didn't arrive at that 100,000 gallons limit by accident: it relates to the Craft Beverage Modernization and Tax Reform Act. This December 2017 US tax concession for small distillers reduced the federal excise tax from $13.50 to $2.70 per proof gallon on the first 100,000 gallons distilled. Initially intended to be temporary, it was made permanent in December 2020 when, seeking to support smaller businesses, President Trump approved a larger package of Covid-19 Relief measures.

But while that legislation is specific to the USA, there's much to like in that definition, not least the emphasis on actual production. I've nothing against third-party bottlers where it's clear what's in the bottle but there have been instances, especially in the USA, of whiskeys that imply they've been distilled by some new, small operation where, in actual fact, they originated in a giant plant in Lawrenceburg, Indiana. Be in no doubt that that company, Midwest Grain Products, makes some very fine products under their own labels but, perfectly legitimately, they sell whiskey to other companies. Regrettably, though, some of them haven't been wholly transparent about where it came from.

But does the distillery have to be 'independently owned' as the ADI would insist? Some large distilling companies have been attracted to the whole idea of craft production and bought stakes in their smaller rivals, or sometimes acquired the whole business. Should that automatically disqualify their products?

Sticking my neck out I'll say not, and as you work your way through the entries you'll find examples of distillers included here who are wholly or partly owned by their larger competitors. Take the Australian Starward as one example, for no better reason than that it appears quite early in these pages. Starward has received backing from Distill Ventures, Diageo's incubator fund (other industry giants have similar vehicles providing venture capital – these are not philanthropic endeavours). There's a very good argument to be made that without their investment and mentorship

Starward simply could not have grown as far and as fast as it has. And without that backing very little of their excellent whisky would have ever made it out of Australia, which would have been the rest of the world's loss.

But the 100,000 proof US gallons of the ADI definition is rather a lot in a smaller marketplace such as the UK, or even the whole of Europe. There are some tiny distilleries where that would represent several years' production. Generally speaking, they're quite happy about their Lilliputian scale and like it that way.

So I contacted the Scottish Distillers Association whose raison d'être is 'promoting the craft of Scottish distilling' and who count amongst their members most of Scotland's smaller distillers of whisky and gin (but none, as far as I could see, of the big ones, who work with the Scotch Whisky Association). They suggested it had previously been set at 'around 100,000 litres' but it seemed that that was no longer an absolute rule.

In summary the meaning of 'craft' is rather vague. Speaking to *The Spirits Business*, a UK drinks industry magazine, Michael Vachon, head of brand development at UK drinks distribution business Maverick Drinks, says it took a lengthy brainstorming session to agree what 'craft' means to him and his team. 'We agreed on six points of craft: craftsmanship, authenticity, quality, provenance, founders and the purpose,' he explains. 'It's more about a set of values to adhere to rather than hard and fast rules. Things we took out of the definitions were probably what we argued over the most, which were first, being independent. We don't think a brand being wholly owned by itself makes it more or less craft. And second, being on a small scale; just because something is small doesn't make it craft.'

So I don't think anyone really knows but, for my part, I'm comfortable with 'craft' as a shorthand portmanteau description of a type of new distillery, generally but not necessarily small in scale and possibly, but again it's not mandatory, independently owned that, importantly for present purposes, might be located anywhere in the world. That's why you'll find whiskies here made in the Big Five producing nations but, as a general rule, they won't be the larger ones and they'll probably be doing something interesting, different or groundbreaking.

In the still house at Koval, Chicago, USA.

One man. . . and some winds of change

Though some of these operations go back a couple of decades, this is for the most part a relatively recent phenomenon, certainly in terms of its visibility and public acceptance. There are several reasons for that but a lot can be laid at the door of one man, Dr James 'Jim' Swan (1941–2017).

More than any one person, Jim Swan influenced the growth and direction of the world whisky movement. He had long and deep experience in Scotch whisky when he launched his own consulting business in 2002, after which he was in constant demand, criss-crossing the globe from Scotland to Taiwan and Israel to Latin America. At the time of his unexpected and sudden death in February 2017 he was probably busier than ever and acknowledged as the go-to guy if you were starting a new distillery or had a problem with an existing one.

His influence may be discerned in the design of the flavour wheel regularly seen in tasting notes and books on whisky; in still design and distilling practice and, above all, in the manufacture and use of casks. In particular, he was a pioneer and advocate of 'shaved, toasted and re-charred' (STR) red-wine casks. That may not seem to be such a big deal but it has had a dramatic impact on the whole world of whisky. Jim Swan's name will crop up time and again in the individual entries here because it's almost impossible to overstate the impact that he has had on the whisky you will drink in the future. A consummate gentleman, he's greatly and sadly missed by all who knew or worked with him.

And other factors have come into play as well: increased consumer interest in whisky, especially single-malt Scotch and small-batch bourbon, and a willingness to pay more for it; greater education and access to information, leading to questioning of the validity and legitimacy of a production hegemony dominated by Scotland; pure entrepreneurial curiosity as to what, for example, a Swedish or Finnish whisky might actually taste like; growing interest in 'artisanal' production, as seen in the rise of farmers' markets and concern for provenance; the availability of small-scale distilling equipment, some marketed as ready for plug-and-play immediate use; and the veritable flood of investment capital, both from venture markets and through crowdfunding as whisky has grown increasingly fashionable. Seen against that backdrop, the explosion of world whisky production seems almost inevitable.

Through various hazards and events we move*

However, as I write, the continuing coronavirus pandemic is putting all operators under severe financial pressure. Many have been able to turn to the production of hand sanitiser, which has been an economic lifeline, and the boom in off-licence sales for consumption at home has provided some relief, though this varies around the world in line with their domestic market's split between on-trade (hotels, pubs, restaurants and so on) and off-trade consumption and local legislation. Many smaller distilleries rely heavily on direct sales to visitors, to whom they can charge their full retail price and so retain all the usual distributor and retailer margins. These are therefore hugely profitable sales (not to mention the valuable direct relationship established with the customer, not least on the various, and increasingly important, social media channels) and this income has been greatly curtailed by the effects of the pandemic. It goes without saying that, across the world, sales to the on-trade have also been very hard hit.

The full impact has yet to be determined but it's my very great fear that by the time this book finds its way into bookshops there will be casualties, though hopefully not amongst the 101. If you're now wondering what you can do to help, the answer is obvious – get online with credit card in hand, and buy, buy, buy!

There is one other, more trivial, effect of coronavirus and that is that onerous travel restrictions since March 2020 have made it impossible for me to visit as many of these distilleries as I would have liked: a scheduled trip to the USA was cancelled at the end of that month and travel has been increasingly difficult ever since. Of course, it's unlikely that I would have ever made it to Argentina or South Africa, and Zoom has helped me meet some really interesting characters and see their set-up, but there were a number in the USA and Europe that I very much wanted to see at first hand. Fortunately, in happier times, from Finland to Taiwan, I have been able to visit a number of these. It's a #firstworldproblem, I do realise that, but a frustration nonetheless that a lot of my work has had to be desk based though, as Dryden reminds us (see footnote), this too shall pass.

The sharp-eyed reader familiar with my previous efforts in *101 World Whiskies to Try Before You Die*, published in 2012 (now rather dated and out of print), and the most recent *101 Whiskies to Try Before You Die* (fourth edition published in 2019)

* John Dryden, after Virgil's *Aeneid*. 'Post varios casus, per tot discrimina rerum.' (1697). But you knew that.

will inevitably notice a small number of entries based on those books. That's because they deserve their place here. I have endeavoured to confirm they remain relevant and corrected for any significant recent change.

Hurry while stocks last. . . or grab it while you can

Sadly for whisky drinkers, the price of almost all whisky has been rising rapidly in recent years and even new distilleries and young whiskies are able to sustain retail prices which would have been thought impossible less than ten years ago. It's our own fault for buying the stuff, I suppose, and we can't blame distillers and retailers for taking profits where they can. Broadly speaking, there are no cheap whiskies any more but there are bargains and, where I can, I've tried to highlight these as well as suggesting a few whiskies that seem to justify some severe damage to your credit card.

In fairness, producing on a small scale is inherently more expensive than making larger volumes, and craft and world whiskies haven't seen the price inflation that has characterised many of the more fashionable Scotch single malts and sought-after small-batch bourbons. Except, that is, for Japan where prices have risen dramatically. I blame the pernicious 'investment' boom for a lot of this but, thankfully, there's not a lot of that type of activity around the whiskies listed here. Generally speaking, they represent very fair value, though we all have our own ideas on what that means.

Something else to consider is the strength of the whisky you're choosing. Normally whisky is sold at 40%, 43% or sometimes 46% abv (alcohol by volume) but it doesn't start out like that. It goes into the barrel at around 65% abv. Evaporation and aging generally mean that it loses strength over time and then it is usually diluted with water prior to bottling. More recently we have seen higher strength whiskies grow in popularity, most notably so-called 'cask strength' bottles – as the name would suggest, these have been bottled as they come from the cask, usually with minimal filtration to remove bits of the charred inside of the barrel. As UK duty is levelled on the alcoholic strength and, quite perniciously, VAT then charged in addition, it stands to reason that all other things being equal a bottle of cask strength whisky will cost more than one at the 40% level; if it helps, try to think of it as offering more bang for your buck. . .

All things, of course, are rarely equal and the trend towards ever more lavish packaging, particularly amongst the more expensive single malts, has also been reflected in higher retail prices. However, relatively few of the whiskies listed here have succumbed to the temptation to gild their respective lilies, for which relief we should all give thanks.

As I'm sure you appreciate, many of the distilleries featured here produce very small quantities that can sell out quickly – in some cases in a matter of hours. So inevitably, you will find availability of particular styles to be patchy at best, and in some cases they may be completely unavailable, but I'd stress that the listing is not necessarily for specific expressions but rather it's the producer to whom I'm drawing attention.

However, some, though not all, of these distilleries have their own online sales operation, or you can scour specialist retailers' websites, or hope that a bottle may turn up in one of the many whisky auction sites that have sprung up in recent years. Or, more fatalistically, you could conclude that while a particular style is now out of reach the distillery concerned will still have something interesting to offer and try that. They certainly won't benefit from secondary sales on auction sites and, if you buy from a current release, it's nice to know that your money has gone to the people responsible rather than some lucky speculator who got in early and is flipping a bottle for a profit.

The scores on the doors. . . or, indeed, the lack of them

Put simply, there aren't any. There are several reasons for this.

Scores are simply one person's opinion – not in my opinion, the opinion of the person that counts here, which is you. I know nothing of your tastes, knowledge, previous whisky experience, budget or other preferred drinks. Apart from the odd 101 gins, I don't drink many other spirits; only the occasional beer and prefer red wines, especially claret and rioja, for pleasure – if you stop to think about it, this must result in a bias in my palate and thus my scores, and the same is true of all other tasters, whether they care to acknowledge it or not.

Scores out of 100 are absurd and ever more so when recorded with decimal points, as is the case in one popular guide. The taster is, in effect, telling us that they can calibrate their score out of 1,000 (which is what the decimal point in a 100 point system indicates). I have my doubts as to the real-world value of such apparent precision which, in my opinion at least, is best ignored.

So too are scores where the taster is brand aware, as they will be for the majority of books. Again, it's a question of bias, albeit an unconscious one. Asked to judge a glass of Glen Whatever, the taster must inevitably call to mind their knowledge of the distillery, recall previous expressions tasted and place the whisky being judged in that wider context. But not here, as this is a score-free zone. Make up your own mind – it's all that matters.

So too for tasting notes. Though there are a few brief impressions here, there has been a tendency in recent years for them to have become ever more extravagant, baroquely detailed and fanciful. Some are quite intimidating – is the aim, one wonders, to guide the reader or to impress him or her with the taster's erudition? Curiously, just as the packaging grows ever more luxurious, there is a further trend for the elaboration to grow in a direct relationship to the price of the whisky under consideration. At their worst, such notes act as a barrier to the neophyte drinker, keen to explore and learn; to suggest that true appreciation comes from membership of an exclusive club, membership of which is obscured by arcane and esoteric rules and procedures.

Whisky doesn't need or benefit from such an approach, which serves to exclude and demean, as does one noted style of tasting notes criticised recently as overtly sexualised, which is crude and off-putting: considering all the above, I believe the space on these pages is better employed not filled with my tasting observations. There is, however, room to accommodate *your* thoughts, and even a score if you choose, so that the book can become a personal reference archive and permanent record of whiskies you have tried.

The enjoyment of whisky should be a broad church, open and welcome to all. As whisky's first true poet put it, the enthusiastic student should taste, learn, and thus informed, judge whisky for themselves with 'his mother wit, his nose and his palate to guide him.*

And, on that note, on to the whiskies!

* Aeneas MacDonald, *Whisky* (1930). May I just add that, in these more enlightened times, that all are equally welcome.

Distilling in a cold climate. Teerenpeli, Lahti, Finland.

1

Distillery	**La Alazana** La Alazana, Las Golondrinas, Chubut, Lago Puelo
Visitor Centre	Yes
Website	www.laalazanawhisky.com

Whisky	
Where	
When	
Verdict	

La Alazana

As I write this, in a state of interminable lockdown, I find myself reflecting that the past few months have been somewhat disagreeable. So perhaps a song* might cheer us up.

> *Don't cry for me, gentle reader*
> *The truth is, I never got there*
> *All through the Covid, its mad persistence*
> *I sent them emails*
> *But kept my distance!*

Sorry about that. Now, back to the book: yes, there are single-malt distilleries in Argentina, three of them apparently, but as La Alazana was the first, so to them goes the honour of representing their country – of which I know little apart from the beguiling rhythm of the tango; the deliciously mouth-watering aroma of fine steak and the voluptuous embrace of their fine, warm red wines. Sadly I've never been, though in writing that sentence I can almost see the wide-open spaces of La Alazana's Patagonian home and taste their drams.

Which, because they were kind enough to send me a sample (the package was opened by some busybody at the UK government's Home Office Border Control who are clearly overwhelmed by work), I can happily endorse as toothsome. It's around six years of age and matured mainly in ex-bourbon barrels with around a quarter in ex-sherry casks. Textbook stuff. Distilling began here in 2011 by a family of farmers, the Serenellis, who, in creating their field-to-bottle distillery, freely acknowledge their respect and love for Scotland. Lila Serenelli even studied for a master's degree at the International Centre for Brewing and Distilling at Edinburgh's Heriot-Watt University and the couple toured Scotland to learn more, though the distillery's robust-looking copper pot stills were built locally to their own design. They grow and then malt local barley and employ Patagonian peat for a tribute to the Islay style, with other expressions using barley sourced from Scotland, though a strong belief in *terroir* is apparent from their scanty website. Currently, and regrettably their whisky isn't available outside Argentina but their pioneering approach more than deserves a place here as illustrative of whisky's increasingly global reach and appeal. Please read on: there are no more songs.

Argentina

2

Distillery

Visitor Centre
Website

Adelaide Hills
Adelaide Hills, Lot.100, Chambers Road,
Hay Valley, South Australia
Yes
www.78degrees.com.au

Whisky

Where

When

Verdict

NATIVE GRAIN
WHISKEY

YEAR 2020
BARREL ADP7
BOTTLE 1/150
CRAFTED BY sacha
700mL   46.2 % ABV

Adelaide Hills

Founded by a former winemaker, this distillery is very new and small, and makes mostly gin. What's more, the minuscule quantities of its whisky (a mere 150 bottles of the most recent release) cost around £250 at current rates. Even if you lived forever you'd probably never taste it.

However, it's here because founder Sacha La Forgia may just be opening a new door for Australian whisky. In any event, he is challenging the conventions about what defines whisky and how it should be made, something worth considering even in the abstract.

Back in 2019, having spent some time thinking about Australia's native grains – once understood and harvested by the native Aboriginal population but now largely ignored – and experimenting with wattleseed, he released the first small batch of Native Grain. Cue outrage and controversy because under Australian whisky regulations wattleseed isn't admitted as grain. Undaunted, he turned to Weeping Grass, which is a cereal and thus acceptable. Now, in one sense, there's nothing extraordinary going on here. People have always distilled what comes to hand – barley in Scotland, maize in the USA, apples in Normandy – so the Native Grain simply asks us to confront the question: 'What would an Australian whisky be like?'

However, the discussion goes beyond that to raise issues around diversity, sustainability and the preservation of indigenous species, which require fewer inputs to flourish in their native environment. Big and important stuff, which La Forgia and his colleagues at the Lot.100 complex are confronting head on as part of a collective seeking 'better liquid, better nourishment, better balance and most of all, sustainability for a better planet'.

So think of his whisky as part of a movement. Longer term there will be more Australian grain whiskies, a deeper and more sustainable relationship with the environment and a more profound sense of *terroir*, which has largely been lost or deliberately ignored in large-scale whisky making. So yes, thought-provoking stuff. That's why it's here and, as we go to print, why 'craft drinks accelerator' Mighty Craft has just acquired Adelaide Hills and a majority stake in the Lot.100 complex. Expansion will doubtless follow so keep watching…

Australia

3

Distillery

Visitor Centre
Website

Archie Rose
Archie Rose Distilling Co.,
Dunning Avenue, Rosebery,
New South Wales and Botany,
Sydney, New South Wales
Yes – at Rosebery distillery
www.archierose.com.au

Whisky	
Where	
When	
Verdict	

DISTILLED, BOTTLED AND SHARED AT

ARCHIE ROSE

DISTILLING CO.

RYE MALT WHISKY

PRODUCT OF SYDNEY, AUSTRALIA

A UNIQUE COMBINATION OF RARE MALTED RYE AND THE FINEST MALTED BARLEY,
PAIRED WITH VIRGIN AMERICAN OAK CASKS AIR-DRIED FOR 36 MONTHS

SPICED CUSTARD, GINGER AND STONE FRUIT WITH A LINGERING HERBAL FINISH

Archie Rose

Remarkably, this business only dates from 2014, but such has been their success that they were able to expand to a new distillery within a few years, starting production at the Botany site in 2020.

However, a certain frisson of controversy surrounds the second Archie Rose distillery in whisky blogging circles, thanks to their patent application for an 'individual malt' process and the installation of cooling jackets on the necks of their pot stills. Or possibly because of their off-the-wall experiments, such as melting huge blocks of ice in a neighbouring restaurant's ironbark wood-fired pizza oven to produce smoked water that they then use to distil their Ironbark Smoked Rye Malt Whisky. Traditionalists might not approve though, conversely, whisky geeks will love the transparency that Archie Rose offer on their website. Under the heading 'Spirit Data' everything about each and every batch of their spirits is laid out in meticulous detail.

Take their Single Malt Whisky, for example. Should you want to know the origin, variety and kiln treatment of each one of the six (yes, six) different malts that were used, it's all here, followed by a precise description of the water and how it was filtered, along with a full account of the brewing and fermentation process. The wash and spirit still charges are laid out along with the complete life story of the 28 casks that made up the second batch of this release. Honestly, I know less about my own children.

Anyway, the good news is that the new distillery represents a substantial expansion so an export drive will doubtless follow with a steady stream of limited and experimental releases of whiskies, gins, rums and other spirits. Those cooling jackets on the whisky stills give incredible flexibility to play tunes on the spirit character, and as long as the temptation to experiment for its own sake is resisted we can expect some intriguing and truly novel results. What's more, with the knowledge gained so freely shared, everyone with eyes can benefit.

However you look at this whisky laboratory, if this is the way world whiskies are going then the whole industry needs to buckle up for an exciting ride. Count me in!

4

Distillery | **Bakery Hill**
Visitor Centre | Bakery Hill, Balwyn North, Victoria
Website | No
| www.bakeryhilldistillery.com.au

Whisky

Where

When

Verdict

Bakery Hill

Right now if you could pick just one hot spot for the development of world whisky, it would probably be the island of Tasmania. So, just to be perverse, Bakery Hill is located north-east of Melbourne in Victoria where they claim to operate 'Australia's premium malt whisky distillery'.

Given that there are, at today's count, rather more than 50 others in production, that's quite some claim – I daresay that Bill Lark (widely considered the founding father of modern Australian whisky) might have something to say, and many of the others do not lack for ambition.

And we might, in passing, note that whisky was being distilled (by Scotland's Distillers Company Ltd of all people) in Australia as early as 1929, although their Corio distillery near Geelong has since closed. Bakery Hill started operations in 2000 and the distillery was enlarged in 2008, allowing larger volumes to be produced and small amounts to be shipped to international markets. Having said that, very little gets out of the state of Victoria, so enthusiastic is the local following. Founder David Baker even took the trouble to telephone late one night to tell me all about the whiskies we can't get, which was thoughtful of him (at least, I think it was kindly meant. . .)

Interestingly, all the output is bottled as single-cask releases, mainly (but not always) at cask strength, so chances are that if you go back for a second bottle it will be different from the one you just finished. Inevitably, given this approach, the small-scale production and the distance it has to travel to European markets, it's not cheap – expect to pay the equivalent of around £90 for a full bottle of the 46% abv versions and more for the cask strength.

What's exciting about this is just how it demonstrates the vibrancy, diversity and willingness to experiment that marks out many of the 'world' distillers; in marked contrast to the rather more staid and proscriptive Scotch whisky industry. As we are about to see, they need to watch out.

Australia

25

5

Distillery	**Belgrove** Belgrove Distillery, 3121 Midland Highway, Kempton, Tasmania
Visitor Centre	No – visits by appointment
Website	www.belgrovedistillery.com.au

Whisky

Where

When

Verdict

BELGROVE
DISTILLERY

RYE WHISKY
100% RYE
NO CHILL FILTRATION

Date bottled 19 / 03 / 2020
Volume 500 mL Alc/Vol 45 %
Approximately 18 standard drinks

This rye was grown, malted,
fermented, distilled, barrelled and
bottled at **Belgrove Distillery**
3121 Midland Highway
Kempton, Tasmania 7030
Distilled by
Peter Bignell.
belgrovedistillery.com.au
Product of Australia

The Gospel

Rye is, if you can forgive their punning website, something of a religion for these guys. Noting that 'early Scotch-Irish settlers in the USA used rye to make whiskey because barley didn't adapt to the North American climate', they've set out 'to reimagine this original American spirit using 100% Australian rye' and, in a very single-minded way have succeeded mightily.

In the beginning there was a love of moonshine and founders Andrew Fitzgerald and US-native Ben Bowles initially launched their venture as Melbourne Moonshine. But whisky grew and an appreciation of classic cocktails – Old Fashioneds and Manhattans – drew the duo to the teasing, spicy notes in rye and the opening of The Gospel distillery in 2019. Selecting a very specific grain from just one farm in the arid Murray Mallee region, and using 100 per cent unmalted rye (note: no other grains, this is righteous Old Testament stuff), Gospel run this through a six-metre-high continuous column still (that's approximately the length of the largest reliably recorded great white shark) of their own design and construction. They then redistil the spirit in a pot still, after which the Straight Rye Whiskey is aged in 24-month-old seasoned barrels for an average of two and a half years, before bottling at 45% abv.

Their second expression is termed Solera Rye and, interestingly, does not carry the designation 'whiskey' on the label. That's because of an unusual maturation regime based on their interpretation of the Spanish solera system: multiple batches are passed through barrels of first-fill American oak, then second- and third-fill American oak, and finally finished in natural wine barrels from the Adelaide Hills. While the oldest stock in the system is more than two years old, the age of the finished product cannot be guaranteed and so what is bottled isn't legally whiskey in Australia (though it would pass muster in the USA).

Impressively for such a small operation, they even work directly with a cooperage in the USA to source new, seasoned American oak from a single forest. Now that's obsessive and indicative of their commitment to their craft.

They also offer a range of four pre-mixed cocktails, which provide the perfect showcase for their ryes. Hallelujah!

Australia

7 Distillery

Visitor Centre
Website

Hellyers Road
Hellyers Road Distillery,
153 Old Surrey Road, Burnie,
Tasmania
Yes
www.hellyersroaddistillery.com.au

Whisky

Where

When

Verdict

Hellyers Road

True story: finding it hard to expand sales of their milk, a group of Tasmanian dairy farmers got together to establish a distillery. And, also true, it's proved a considerable success. The first whisky was produced in 2006 and until the development of Great Southern Distilling and Starward, now greatly assisted by Diageo's money and expertise, burst onto the scene, Hellyers Road was probably Australia's largest craft distillery. With a capacity of around 100,000 litres per annum, it remains a significant force on the Tasmanian scene.

They were also early and energetic exporters, shipping today to Japan and more than 20 European markets. So it's a very good place to start your exploration of Australian – sorry, *Tasmanian* – whiskies, especially as the brand offers a decent range of single malts at up to 15 years of age along with the more limited, and consequently hard to find and accordingly expensive, Master Series.

Much like their fellow island distilleries, malted barley is obtained from Hobart's Cascade Brewery, but the house style diverges somewhat from their competitors, possibly due to the fact that reconstituted bourbon casks from Jack Daniel's are favoured for maturation, providing a distinctive vanilla note on the palate. However, a glance at the range reveals a peated variant and the use of a highly rated Pinot Noir cask finishing so nothing is lacked for variety. All expressions are non-chill filtered and free from any added colouring.

The distillery is also notable for employing stainless steel in the body of both the large pot stills, presumably due to the dairy influence, although copper is used for the heads, necks and lyne arms.

Today, Master Distiller Mark Littler presides over an operation that, as well as distilling, includes a café and visitor centre – like many others, tourism has proved an increasingly important source of income and around 40,000 visitors are received here annually.

Finally, turns out Mr Hellyer was a nineteenth-century explorer and cartographer who, according to local legend, had little more than a bullock gang and the most basic of tools to build the trail that became the road that is home to the distillery that today is named in his honour.

8

Distillery
Visitor Centre
Website

The Lark
The Lark Distillery, Hobart, Tasmania
Yes – escorted one- and two-day tours
www.larkdistillery.com

Whisky	
Where	
When	
Verdict	

The Lark

Bill Lark, of the eponymous distillery, is a cheerful fellow. As well he might be. He's pretty much the father of modern Australian whisky and, if today he is taking life a little slower as more of a Brand Ambassador than CEO, he can look back with pride on a considerable and influential legacy that has stretched far beyond his native shores.

Apart from his own operation, he even helped found the Tasmanian Whisky Producers Association. With more than 40 active members, it's the best possible demonstration of the vibrant craft-distilling scene that has taken root on Tasmania since Bill first set up in 1992 and revived an industry dormant since 1838, when Lady Jane Franklin persuaded her Governor husband that distilling should be shut down. 'I would prefer barley be fed to pigs than it be used to turn men into swine,' she's alleged to have told him. Perhaps she preferred vodka – history does not relate.

Today an enthusiastic young team looks after the day-to-day production. The original site, on Hobart's waterfront, remains a shop front, with café, retail outlet and whisky bar, while the 'new' distillery in Cambridge about 20 minutes away has grown significantly. Their property now includes their own peat bog and cooperage.

For a while a few years ago The Lark was shipping to international markets. Sadly, more recently, the supply has dwindled as their limited production is largely snapped up in Australia. So why mention it?

Well, to acknowledge Bill Lark's place on the world whisky scene and – roll of drums, please – the very real possibility that supplies to Europe may well have resumed by the time this book hits the shelves. In a little bit of Tasmanian devilry the distillery hinted to me that 'we don't have any presence in Europe at the moment but certainly intend to'. Let's hope it's not too long before they're back and when you see some, just grab it.

Australia

9

Distillery	**Limeburners**
	Great Southern, Albany, Western Australia
Visitor Centre	Yes
Website	www.distillery.com.au

Whisky
Where
When
Verdict

GREAT SOUTHERN DISTILLING COMPANY

Limeburners

Small Batch   *Hand Distilled*   *Non Chill Filtered*

western australian
Single Malt Whisky

—American Oak—

43% Alc/Vol   Product of Australia   700mL

Limeburners

I felt it only fair to include something from Western Australia. After all, Australia's a big place – this whisky's home in Albany is around 1,600 miles from the nearest distilling cluster in Adelaide. But Albany's home to something big and important: Limeburners' owner, Great Southern Distilling Company, was the first to distil whisky (well, legally that is) in Western Australia. In 2004, founder Cameron Syme set himself the simple if immodest goal of making the best spirits in the world. And, to be fair, the boy's done good, collecting a number of major awards along the way.

He now operates three distilleries, one of which is dedicated to gin, but two produce whisky, including (look away now if ophidiophobic) Dugite, Tiger Snake and Rye of the Tiger. But the first, and still the most significant, expression is called Limeburners, which is to be found in a variety of different releases. Fortunately Great Southern are active exporters, sending their products to the US and the UK. At the time of writing, The Whisky Exchange (one of the better on-line UK-based retailers) held stock.

What you won't find are whiskies with specific age statements, as Great Southern are quite clear that their ethos is not to work to ages but state unambiguously that 'the whisky is ready only when it's ready'. This was Syme's position from the outset and it seems to be working for them to this day.

All the Limeburner whiskies are unashamedly expensive with the flagship Directors Cut sitting close to £250 for a standard bottle, albeit at 61% abv. With that price tag you might consider starting your exploration of their range with the sub-£100 American Oak. It's unpeated, while the pricier releases generally employ locally sourced peat for a more forceful smokier style.

Their Heavy Peat certainly wowed judges at the American Distilling Institute's 2020 awards, collecting all sorts of accolades, including carrying off the International Smoked Whisky Trophy and being declared Best International Craft Whisky. These ADI awards are keenly contested so, if you like a peated whisky, this could be the one for you.

Just get ready for some damage to your credit card.

Australia

10

Distillery
Visitor Centre
Website

Overeem
Sawford Distillery, Hobart, Tasmania
No
www.overeemwhisky.com

Whisky

Where

When

Verdict

Overeem

Tracking the twists and turns of Australian craft distilling, the history of the Overeem brand and trademark is somewhat too complex to relate here but after a number of changes of ownership it's back, more or less, with the founding family. Casey Overeem first set up at the Overeem distillery in Huntingdon in 2007 but sold out to Lark Distillery in 2014. After Lark sold the name, some of the original stock was bought back by his daughter Jane and her husband Mark Sawford, with the semi-retired Casey in charge of the Overeem tasting panel, mentoring in production and turning out at events and tastings as Brand Ambassador.

Today, distilling is at the new Sawford Distillery and is the responsibility of Mark Sawford, assisted by Nicole Harris. Sawford distillery whiskies are anticipated from 2022 so what's currently available comes from the original Overeem production which, like many of its counterparts, was extremely limited. This, along with the fact that many are released at cask strength and thus incur the penalty of higher duty, accounts for the relatively high retail price.

What's more interesting though is the Overeem commitment to releasing exclusively as single-cask bottling, either at 43% or 60% abv and their use of specially re-coopered 100-litre casks, be they former bourbon, port or sherry. Through the greater interaction of spirit and wood the smaller cask size promotes more rapid maturation and this, combined with the Tasmanian climate, means the whisky is typically fully matured at between 5 and 7 years. Some reports suggest that larger bourbon and sherry barrels may have been filled, presumably for longer aging.

Locally grown Franklin barley is used, around 50 per cent of the mash having been lightly peated. But this is Tasmanian peat, of course, and just as Ardbeg's Islay peat differs from Highland Park's Orcadian variety so Tasmanian peat adds its own distinct note of gum trees and local grasses. As regular readers will know, I'm not the greatest fan of heavy peating but this seems to me to lend a more delicate, almost ethereal air to the nose and palate.

Or that could be the power of suggestion and I could just be drifting dangerously close to the pretensions of wine writing. You try it and decide for yourself.

Australia

11

Distillery

Visitor Centre
Website

Starward
New World Whisky Distillery,
Melbourne, Victoria
No
www.starward.com.au

Whisky	
Where	
When	
Verdict	

Starward

Given that Diageo is the world's largest maker of Scotch whisky (and no minnow in the Irish or bourbon categories either) you wouldn't think they'd need to invest in a small Australian distillery. But they did – to the tune of Au$ 10 million if rumours are to be believed – and, at a stroke, put this 2008 start-up into a position front and centre as the global representative of Australian whisky.

Lots of people sought backing from Diageo's venture-capital fund, but as the folks responsible for writing the cheques saw it at the time (because I asked them), they felt Starward was 'adding to and enhancing the world of whisky' and brought a 'compelling ambition for global scale [with] the right mix of skills, perseverance and ability to stay optimistic, ride those waves and to keep driving forward'.

That was back in 2016. So have Starward met those ambitious and demanding requirements? Well, first off they had Diageo's cash to build up their stocks and then, in 2020, significantly expand capacity. As just one example, the new wash still has around four times the capacity of the old one, which has been repurposed as the new, enlarged spirit still, and you can now find a decent number of their whiskies in the UK and the US at very acceptable prices.

So, to give them the fair go their efforts deserve, you'd have to conclude that Starward have lived up to their stellar billing. They pioneered the use of Australian wine and 'apera' casks – apera is the new Sunday name for Aussie fortified wine or Australian sherry, as it was known in the bad old days – and given the world-beating quality of the best wines from Down Under that's a great place for any new-make spirit to spend its days in Melbourne's 'four seasons in a day' climate.

You could, at a pinch, just grab any one of their bottles but I'd recommend starting with their Solera expression. Made from Australian malted barley and aged in those apera casks, it's rich, sweetly warming, deceptively full and complex for its comparative youth, and surprises you on the finish with some sprightly spice notes that mingle deliciously with dark orange chocolate. Reminds you of Christmas in fact.

Australia

12

Distillery	**Sullivans Cove**
	Sullivans Cove Distillery, Cambridge, Tasmania
Visitor Centre	Yes
Website	www.sullivanscove.com

Whisky	
Where	
When	
Verdict	

Sullivans Cove

This was the very first Australian whisky I ever tried and it left the abiding impression that this was not a product that was going to trouble anyone. But that was many years ago now and, to be fair, I should quickly acknowledge that things have moved on at a number of levels. This is a completely different operation from the early days, so read on.

New owners took control in 1999, the distillery was relocated to the present site in 2004 and the initial run of whisky was quietly swept under the carpet. What they sell today, under the Sullivans Cove name, has improved out of all recognition and, from 2007, international awards started to flow. In 2014 one of their bottlings was declared World's Best Single Malt at the World Whisky Awards, which somewhat immodest (and now rather dated) claim they continue to feature strongly

Right now, Sullivans Cove can be found in quite a few international markets, although, if you live in Australia, you can also buy and hold your own cask. If the distillery keeps progressing and winning awards, this may prove a shrewd buy for the enthusiast.

At the heart of their core range is the Double Cask, which has been improved enormously in recent years, albeit at the cost of a rather alarming increase in price. Launched at 40% abv, recent batches are aged longer and bottled at higher strengths, representing a marriage of ten different casks, ranging in age from 11 to 17 years. As well as whisky from several American oak ex-bourbon casks, this might involve both American and French oak casks, which have been previously used for either tawny port, white or red wine.

The distillery also offers American and French Oak matured expressions, as well as Single Cask releases, limited editions and selections of their Old and Rare bottlings, all at quite premium prices. Here in the UK, when you can find them, these bottlings fetch over £1,000 which is pretty rich meat by any standards,

In a wry glance to Tasmania's darker past as a penal colony, they style their whisky: 'Distilled with Conviction'. It's certainly no crime to drink it, but check your bank balance first!

Australia

13

Distillery

Visitor Centre
Website

Whipper Snapper
Whippersnapper Distillery,
139 Kensington Street, East Perth,
Western Australia
Yes
www.whippersnapperdistillery.com

Whisky	
Where	
When	
Verdict	

Whipper Snapper

While a good number of Australian distillers have embraced a style deeply influenced by Scotland's single malts, a few have had the audacity to break away from that colonial heritage and look elsewhere. With Australia being a significant market for American whiskeys, especially Jack Daniel's, firms such as Belgrove (see 5) and The Gospel (see 6) have turned to the USA for inspiration.

But, to be completely honest with you, I started to check out Whipper Snapper on the basis of their funky name. And then, what name came up? Why, none other than that of Frank McHardy, late of Springbank and a copper-bottomed, gilt-edged, tip-top whisky legend who today may be found as an adviser to start-up distilleries. And here he is.

So I had to dig deeper, as Whipper Snapper are dedicated to making a bourbon-style product. However, as their 'Whisky Magician' (I imagine he's embarrassed by that), Frank is advising on single-malt recipes, process and maturation, clearly there's some work in progress – something which we can anticipate with more than normal eagerness. Meanwhile, founders Jimmy McKeown and Alasdair Malloch have not been idle and are clearly ready to challenge orthodoxy, with a range that includes Wheat and Project Q Quinoa Whiskey; Jetpack Hard Coffee and various moonshines, available in white, barrel-aged and several flavours. Essentially these are prototypes from the distillery's opening years, while waiting for fully aged whiskey.

But the initial vision and current heart of the project is Upshot, a bourbon style, using West Australian corn, wheat and malted barley (80 per cent corn, 10 per cent each of wheat and malt), all destined for their column still and freshly charred American oak barrels. Crazy Uncle Moonshine gets six weeks' maturation, but their signature Upshot Australian Whiskey enjoys two full years.

Their logo of a World War 2 bomber nods to a heritage of moonshine distilling from two war veterans – a pilot from the USA and the other an Aussie native – who shared tales and a recipe with Alasdair Malloch. But he and his co-pilot are aiming high in what they describe as the 'relentless pursuit to create the perfect Australian whisky. . .[handcrafting] a range of premium, authentic craft whiskeys that are set to redefine our perception and inspire a new generation. . . using 100% local West Australian grains and highlighting innovation and sustainability'.

Australia

14

Distillery
Visitor Centre
Website

Reisetbauer
Reisetbauer, Kirchdorfergut
No – visits by appointment
www.reisetbauer.at

Whisky
Where
When
Verdict

HANS

HANSI JUN.

REISETBAUER & SON

AGED **12** YEARS
SINGLE MALT WHISKY

**HANS REISETBAUER GEHT SEINEN EIGENEN WEG –
VOM HOLZFASS BIS ZUM QUELLWASSER!**

Das Besondere am Reisetbauer 'n Son Single Malt
Whisky ist zum einen die sorgfältige Auswahl
der Holzfässer befreundeter Winzer und zum
anderen das reine und unbelastete Quellwasser
einer Mühlviertler Alm.

Reisetbauer

With its long-standing heritage of small-scale fruit distilling, Austria has embraced whisky with enthusiasm. Today there are at least a dozen small distilleries making whisky, though generally on a pretty modest scale and more as a sideline to their fruit brandies. However, though their production is limited and the whiskies hard to find I thought I should pick one, if only as further proof that whisky is spreading round the world, frequently alongside other noble distilling traditions.

Reisetbauer got the nod as they've been making whisky since 1995 and are therefore amongst the very first pioneers of Austrian whisky and, having shrewdly reserved some casks for extended maturation, can offer their single malt at 7, 12 and 15 Years Old. And, just as an aside, they're very attractively packaged.

It's a father-and-son operation where owner Hans Reisetbauer has collected Austria's Falstaff Spirits Trophy on numerous occasions and has been named Austria's best distiller, so presumably is confident about his whisky. In any event, they stress that they are not trying to ape the style of Scotch but produce a distinctly Austrian take on whisky, using locally grown winter malting barley from the nutrient-rich soils around Kirchdorfergut.

It's a vivid demonstration of their commitment to long-term quality that Reisetbauer started distilling malt in 1995, but the first bottles weren't released until 2002. Former wine casks that previously held Chardonnay and *trockenbeerenauslese* casks are employed for all three aged expressions.

Wine casks are no longer the novelty that once they were in whisky but a word about *trockenbeerenauslese*, which is not a frequently seen cask type. But once you understand that this describes a style of sweet dessert wine where the grapes have been picked by hand, one at a time, after they have been affected by 'noble rot' (*Botrytis cinerea*) you will appreciate that these casks are both rare and pricey.

The style resembles a particularly intense Sauternes or ice wine, but before you grab a bottle, be aware that most *trockenbeerenauslese* wines are very expensive. For once, it may actually be cheaper to stick to whisky but, like its fellow countrymen, Reisetbauer may be hard to find. It's one to schnapp up (sorry).

Austria

15

Distillery
Visitor Centre
Website

Belgian Owl
The Owl Distillery, Grâce-Hollogne
Yes
www.belgianwhisky.com

Whisky

Where

When

Verdict

Belgian Owl

First a word on the distillery itself, which is located in some handsome old buildings near Liège. It is, I think, almost unique in first making whisky in a century-old vintage mobile still. Unusual, but there is, to this day, a tradition in mainland Europe of travelling distillers who take their equipment on a trailer to small farms to distil fruit spirits and *eau de vie*. Much Armagnac is produced in this way, though such a tradition never took root in Scotland. It's a mouth-watering thought that potentially every small farmer in Britain could look out at a field of their own barley (or, indeed, their own orchards or raspberry cages) and contemplate drinking their produce.

Eventually this particular peripatetic alembic found a home in what is Belgium's first whisky producer. Production was boosted with the installation of two smaller pot stills from Switzerland but, with demand increasing and a number of rivals opening up, the Owl now has a permanent roost using some old Scottish stills.

These stills have a great pedigree, having come in 2013 from Speyside where they had worked at Caperdonich. This had closed in 2002 and the equipment was sold. Refurbished and somewhat remodelled by renowned Rothes still makers Forsyths, the stills live again and have allowed Belgian Owl to greatly increase production and sales.

So is this Belgian whisky, or a strangely mutated Scotch? Firmly Belgian I'd have to say: the barley is harvested from fields adjacent to the distillery and they are at pains to stress that 'our philosophy, our choices and our values define our distillery and our whisky' and the pride they take in 'promoting our local area whilst respecting each stage of the production'.

Everything is matured in first-fill ex-bourbon casks and the whisky is neither coloured nor chill filtered. Currently there are also a number of extra aged expressions and limited editions, some at cask strength.

Founder Etienne Bouillon and his original partners are one of the increasingly diverse group of enthusiasts who have challenged the established wisdom that great whisky can only be made in the 'classic' whisky nations and who have followed their enthusiasm to make a dream come true. What's more, this dream had wheels.

Belgium

16

Distillery

Visitor Centre
Website

Glen Breton
Glenora, Glenville, Inverness,
Nova Scotia
Yes
www.glenoradistillery.com

Whisky

Where

When

Verdict

Glen Breton

Rare

North America's First
Single Malt Whisky

Canadian/Canadien

Aged Years **14** Ans d'âge

43% alc./vol. 750mL

Glen Breton

Though relatively little known outside North America, Canada is a significant whisky producer with a long history and home to many fine whiskies. For a long time it was dominated by a few very large producers who tended to concentrate on the Canadian and US markets, but today they are looking outwards and the flowering of smaller distilling operations justifies a long-overdue reappraisal of Canadian whisky.

But, just to be clear, Glen Breton is not from Scotland. A bottle reading 'North America's First Single Malt Whisky' and bearing a large red maple leaf on the front, together with the words 'Canadian/Canadien' prominently displayed probably makes that clear, though it was the cause of a lengthy and expensive legal battle with the Scotch Whisky Association which the Scots eventually lost in the Canadian Supreme Court. So in theory, you can now buy Canadian Single Malt Whisky in Scotland. However, it does seem very hard to find outside of North America.

Glen Breton were genuine pioneers, true innovators when their Rare 8 Year Old came onto the market. Back then they leant heavily on Scottish expertise and equipment, with Bowmore advising on distilling and much of the original plant being supplied from Scotland. Since then, a more distinctly Canadian personality has emerged but their achievement is still a quite remarkable one and I don't feel they've ever really got full credit for it, especially when the number of single malts now produced on that continent are fully considered. It may look obvious today but a Canadian single malt was a bold venture back in 1990.

Despite the distillery remaining quite modest in scale they've gone on to offer Glen Breton Rare as 10, 14, 19, 21 and 25 Year Old expressions along with the first single malt finished in ice-wine barrels from the nearby Jost Vineyards. Understandably, the older expressions are extremely limited in number.

You can also commission your own 55-gallon* cask or, when you visit to check how it's maturing, stay at their inn or the other accommodation that's available on site.

Canada

---

* These would be Imperial gallons, of course, as opposed to the smaller US gallons of their southern neighbours.

17

Distillery Stalk & Barrel
Visitor Centre Still Waters Distillery, Concord, Ontario
Website No
www.stillwatersdistillery.com

Whisky

Where

When

Verdict

STALK & BARREL

— EST. 2009 —

ART
SCIENCE
PASSION

THREE
BARREL
WHISKY

43.0% alc./vol.

750ml

CT OF CANADA   S&B   PRODUIT DU C

Stalk & Barrel

The Still Waters distillery claims the distinction of being Ontario's first small-batch distillery, something not so very remarkable in the current era but pioneering for its day, which was as recently as 2009. They opened with a vodka, which they still make, but joint founders Barry Stein and Barry Bernstein always had whisky in their sights and laid down the first casks of their single malt within the same year.

Initially aiming to emulate single-malt Scotch their attention also turned to other grains and they began experimenting with corn, rye and wheat. The local Ontario rye that they selected turned out to give exceptional results and the first 100% Rye Whisky, released in 2014, really established Stalk & Barrel's reputation. Production of their single malt continues and they have gone on to release two blends using malted barley, rye and corn, imaginatively named Blue Blend, Red Blend, and the more recent Pink and Green Spotted Blend (actually it's Three Barrel Whisky – they're nothing if not strictly literal in their approach).

Don't be fooled by the modest pricing. While greatly valued by those in the know (that includes you now), Canadian whiskies are still to achieve wider recognition. The country's long tradition of distilling had been somewhat devalued by the historic legacy of Prohibition, when the pursuit of volume and low prices for the neighbouring US market took priority over careful aging and quality. However, those days of doleful memory are being rapidly and rightly left behind thanks to a new generation of smaller distillers and to the energetic promotion of his country's production by writer Davin de Kergommeaux, whose books have prompted a new appreciation of Canadian distilling.

Today Ontario alone boasts over 30 craft distillers and its own Craft Distillers Association (OCDA), an indication of how vibrant and fast-growing this sector has become. From presenting the newcomers with the bewildering and labyrinthine regulations that met the Still Waters Distillery, the local government now actively promote their craft distilleries via the state-controlled Liquor Control Board of Ontario which holds an effective monopoly of spirit retailing (readers from outside North America may be surprised to learn that the state determines which whisky or other spirit you can drink – a similar system exists in the 17 'control states' of the USA).

Now offering contract distilling and consultancy services, these still waters run deep.

Canada

18

Distillery

Visitor Centre
Website

Victoria Caledonian
Macaloney's Caledonian Distillery
& Twa Dogs Brewery, Saanich,
Greater Victoria, B.C.
Yes
www.victoriacaledonian.com

Whisky	
Where	
When	
Verdict	

MACALONEY'S
CALEDONIAN

❧ GLENLOY ❧
ISLAND SINGLE MALT WHISKY

WHISKYMAKER'S SIGNATURE EXPRESSION

ALC./ VOL.	PPM SCALE	BOTTLE Nº	BOTTLED ON	KENTUCKY BOURBON, RECHARRED, RED WINE & SHERRY CASKS
46%	0	BS 11196	01/21	

750 mL
NATURAL COLOUR
NON-CHILL FILTERED   WHISKYMAKER

Victoria Caledonian

Imagine you've walked into a building with CALEDONIAN DISTILLERY slapped across the fascia; you see some familiar pot stills carrying the famous Forsyths branding; your guide is kilted and in the background you can hear a gentleman with a broad Scottish accent. So you might be forgiven for thinking you were in Scotland. But, in fact, you'd be around 4,500 miles from Edinburgh airport where your journey might have started, on Vancouver Island in British Columbia, Canada. It's here that Dr Graeme Macaloney persuaded 270 Canadian investors and the Canadian taxpayer to advance around Can$ 10 million to build what he told them was destined to become 'the finest single malt whisky in North America'. And, while he was about it, a craft brewery into the bargain. He's the ex-pat Scot you could hear expounding on the delivery of this remarkable vision. Fortunately he knows a thing or two about venture capital, not to mention fermentation science and technology.

But he didn't do it alone. His development team comprised Dr Jim Swan (who we met first in the Introduction and shall meet again) and long-time Diageo Master Distiller Mike Nicolson, experienced in some of Scotland's finest distilleries. With their combined expertise the Caledonian Distillery was up and running by the middle of 2016 and very soon attracting positive reviews and a cask-full of awards. Many new start-ups have come to rely on tourism and gin for essential cash flow while their whisky matures. Victoria Caledonian certainly welcomes visitors, including many of their crowdfunder supporters, but instead of gin have turned to craft brewing for additional income. That's logical because, in essence, a distillery is basically a brewery with some stills at one end.* Today, thanks to Dr Swan's expert advice on maturation, Macaloney Distillers already offer a considerable range of their Island Malts or you can buy into their customisable cask programme and, with a little bit of help, design your very own whisky.

With their Glenloy and Invermallie expressions now launched, these are unquestionably whiskies with big hopes and dreams about which you will certainly hear more before long.

STOP PRESS: Notwithstanding their ignominious defeat at the hand of Glen Breton (see 16), the Scotch Whisky Association have now challenged much of Victoria Caledonian's branding. Mark my words, this won't end well.

Canada

---

* Did you know that in many distilleries the assistant manager's job title was brewer? Now you know why.

19

Distillery | **Stauning**
Visitor Centre | Stauningvej 38, Skjern
Website | Yes
 | www.stauningwhisky.com

Whisky

Where

When

Verdict

Stauning

If there's a moral here, it's might just be 'be careful what you wish for'. The nine friends who in 2005, on something of a whim, decided to make some whisky probably didn't hope or expect that ten years later they would be managing a £10-million investment from Diageo's incubator fund. Or that they would take Danish whisky onto the world stage, via the internationally renowned Noma restaurant. Or scale up from two to 24 stills, while still striving to maintain the consistent quality that excited writers and bloggers pretty much from day one.

Now they have a 900,000-litre distillery to run. That's not large by Scottish standards but it's *big* on the world scene and *HUGE* for Denmark. Very soon that whisky will start to reach maturity, hence the recent decision to commission new labels and bottles that move them from boutique operation 50cl to the industry standard 70cl. Stauning is coming of age.

It's been a remarkable achievement by any lights, particularly as they insist on sticking with their small stills, direct firing and open-floor maltings to prepare only locally grown grains often dried over locally harvested peat.

Smoky whisky is what they're best known for and how they established their reputation. Understandably, then, they make great play of this on the excellent and very detailed website suggesting that their Smoke is 'a thoroughbred *terroir* whisky'.

However, there is considerably more here, including rye and barley variants, Kaos (rye and malt blend) and Bastard, finished in mescal casks. A peek into the warehouse would also reveal experiments: casks which have held cognac, Calvados, or vermouth. While some would be permitted under the regulations for Scotch whisky, Stauning benefit from greater freedom to innovate and see what works for their spirit. It's definitely a gauntlet thrown down to whisky's old world though again, I doubt if anyone intended that in the early days in the back room of an old butcher's shop.

The new distillery is a dramatic statement – a fine modern building of clean, crisp lines that respects the Danish architectural vernacular yet has its own distinct character. Having come this far in just 15 years, it's exciting to imagine what Stauning will be doing by 2035.

Denmark

20

Distillery Thy Whisky
Visitor Centre Thy Whisky, Gyrup, Snedsted
Website Yes
www.thy-whisky.dk

Thy Whisky

Whisky

Where

When

Verdict

Thy Whisky

Thy Whisky – not as the name might lead you to conclude *Your Whisky*, but in acknowledgement of the Thy region where the distillery is located – is another instance of distilling returning to its farming roots. After all, what is distilling in its essence other than a method of turning a bulky, relatively low-value and perishable crop such as barley or another cereal into a high-value product that can be easily stored and transported, isn't prone to rapid spoilage and doesn't attract vermin (bloggers excepted)?*

So for the seventh-generation farmer Nicolaj Nicolajsen it seemed a wholly natural move to experiment with heritage grain varieties sourced from the Nordic Seed Bank. With the help of distiller Anders Bilgram from the Nordisk Brænderi distillery, he began with an old Nordic barley strain, Imperial (rather as some Scottish distilleries have trialled the use of bere barley from Orkney). Since 2010, everything here has been grown on the family farm where they have created a wholly organic, single-estate distilling operation, significantly expanded over the years as word spread worldwide of this intriguing experiment in *terroir*. In 2017, Nicolajsen handed over the reins to his daughters as the business grew to embrace the family's eighth generation. Today, even malting is carried out here, making it viable to develop small-batch releases from a variety of grains, some landrace varieties and some more modern strains for the distillery's own use and to sell to other small Danish distillers. Indeed, there are now at least a baker's dozen in active production.

The principal expressions, all simply packaged and modestly priced, are produced and released in distinct batches and identified by number, comprising Fjordboen (sherry-cask matured), Stovt (caramel malts with both bourbon and port casks, finished in barrels previously used for stout), Bøg (beechwood smoked malt) and the heritage-grain variety Kornmod. Alongside these, Thy Whisky also offer distillery exclusives including a rye whisky based on spelt and white spirit, showing themselves open to innovation and experimentation.

The visitor centre runs a limited operation with English-language tours offered on Wednesdays in July and August.

Denmark

21

Distillery

Visitor Centre
Website

Adnams
Copper House Distillery, Southwold,
Suffolk
Yes
www.adnams.co.uk

Whisky	
Where	
When	
Verdict	

Adnams

We don't hear too much about Adnams on the world whisky scene, which is rather a shame: the whiskies are rather good and excellent value to boot. However, I suppose that if you've been brewing great beer since 1872 and operate more than 70 pubs and an off-licence chain in your own Suffolk backyard, then your own outlets provide a ready market for a necessarily limited production that's split between vodka, gin and a range of liqueurs before we get to the time-consuming business of making whisky.

But, as you'd expect from their reputation as brewers, they've made a pretty decent job of it. (I've also tasted their gin, which is excellent; I haven't the faintest idea about the vodka as I have a special dispensation never to touch the stuff.)

The equipment was all new and state-of-the-art when installed in 2009, which is one advantage of starting from scratch, with decent capital behind you. At the time, Adnams were first in the UK to combine a brewery and a distillery on the same premises, challenging a somewhat arcane old law which previously prevented this, and they are keen to stress their energy and water efficiencies and the fact that their rye comes from fields close to the distillery.

The Single Malt was launched as long ago as 2013 and they've since added to the range with a Rye Malt, with a healthy 75 per cent rye mash bill (that's the mix of cereals), and a distinctive Triple Malt, using wheat, barley and oats. At 47% abv this packs a punch and, as I've implied, I don't really feel they've ever had full credit for their innovation and great pricing.

If you get the chance to visit them at their charmingly traditonal English seaside home, you definitely should grab it and not let go. After you've enjoyed a tour of the brewery and distillery Southwold itself is quite charming; the beach huts are fun to ogle (especially after you realise the prices) and the pier is worth the trip on its own if only for the delightfully eccentric collection of amusement machines created by the oddball inventor Tim Hunkin. Sitting on Southwold beach, English single malt in hand, is one of the great pleasures in life.

England

22

Distillery
Visitor Centre
Website

Bimber
Bimber Distillery, 56 Sunbeam Road, Park Royal, London
Yes
www.bimberdistillery.co.uk

Whisky	
Where	
When	
Verdict	

Bimber

Gosh! The Bimber distillery has a dedicated floor malting at Britain's oldest maltsters, wooden washbacks, their own on-site cooperage, direct-fired stills and use barley grown to their own specification from a single, named farm. All this on a industrial estate in London's 'glamorous' Park Royal, roughly halfway between Diageo's global centre for world domination and the notorious Wormwood Scrubs prison (exercising great restraint I am eschewing the obvious opportunity for some witty quip in the belief that the reader will wish to insert their own *bon mot*).

All Bimber's attention to detail and tradition sounds dangerously obsessive and I do observe with some concern that on their otherwise excellent website they have a Klub (sic) for 'like-minded individuals' and an alarming propensity to the p-word.

But much may be forgiven in their neophytic enthusiasm.

Bimber, which is the Polish for moonshine, was set up in 2015 by Dariusz Plazewski and Ewelina Chruszczyk. And they, as you might guess, are Polish. Dariusz, having learnt the distiller's arts from his father and grandfather, isn't actually a beginner, though he's most certainly an enthusiast, determined to do things right as he sees it.

Actually, it *is* obsessive and there are so many little details about the finer points of distillation at Bimber that it would become tedious to list them even if I had space: crushed grains in the mill, rather than shredded husks; extremely long fermentation times; pre-toasted oak for the washbacks which they built themselves and so on, right through the process. They even redesigned the stills to get more copper contact and lighter, fruitier flavours.

Actually, I must mention the casks because Bimber insist on ex-bourbon, with a soupçon of American virgin oak and ex-sherry wood, sourced from a real, actual solera in Jerez.

None of this was cheap but, all things considered and taking the bottling strength into account, it represents incredible value. Get some now before more people realise that this tiny distillery crammed into a north-west London industrial shed is taking single-malt whisky by the throat and setting standards that should embarrass half of Scotland.

If you haven't got the picture by now, check out the rave reviews on social media and blog sites. It's not just me.

England

23

Distillery

Visitor Centre
Website

Cotswolds
Cotswolds Distillery, Stourton,
Shipston-on-Stour
Yes
www.cotswoldsdistillery.com

Whisky	
Where	
When	
Verdict	

Cotswolds

Located in the heart of the English countryside in a rather lovely distillery in a charmingly bucolic setting, Cotswolds is a poster boy for the new wave of English distilling and really quite as lovely as you'd imagine. The level of investment here – on distillery, offices and visitor centre, packaging, not to mention the youthful and enthusiastic team – is impressive. And they have taken this legacy around the world, with one of the initial distilling team now making a distinctive Japanese gin.

The operation was established by former hedge-fund trader and ex-banker Daniel Szor. (He's even gone and written a book now! Is there no end to his talents? *Spirit Guide: In Search of an Authentic Life*. Interesting read – buy one.) He abandoned the City to follow his dream of making whisky with locally grown and malted barley. Good idea but it takes time and money, hence the various crowdfunding campaigns that Cotswolds launched, along with some excellent gin.

However, since 2017 they've released various whisky expressions and very good they are too, by George – or rather, by Jim.

That's because we can detect the hand of the late Dr Jim Swan who advised on aspects of production and maturation, and in particular on cask selection. Fortunately, they listened to what he had to say and the result is a huge success and a credit to all involved. The initial releases, especially the Founder's Choice, were excellent and have only improved with additional aging and different barrel finishes.

Their tasty Sherry Cask single malt is a great example. Under Swan's early influence, Cotswolds have brought together American and Spanish oak hogsheads and butts, some seasoned with dry oloroso sherry and others with sweet, raisiny Pedro Ximénez. Naturally quantities are limited and each annual batch release will vary, reflecting their full sherry-aged maturation, allowing the whisky to develop a full and rather creamy flavour of dark stone fruits with hints of roasted almonds, followed by peppery oak spice.

What's more, being bottled at cask strength it's really excellent value and rather handsomely presented. A great souvenir from a visit to a fine exemplar English distillery.

England

24

Distillery

Visitor Centre
Website

East London
East London Liquor Company,
Bow Wharf, London
Yes
www.eastlondonliquorcompany.com

Whisky

Where

When

Verdict

EAST
LONDON
LIQUOR CO.

WHISKY

CASK AGED IN:
VIRGIN
FRENCH OAK
CHESTNUT
ŠTR SHERRY
BOURBON

RN005

LONDON
RYE®

70CL
47.2%VOL

East London

Here's another in the new wave of distilleries who have regenerated a proud tradition and brought distilling back to our capital.

And capital stuff it is, based around some serious German stills where they make vodka, rum, gin and English whisky. The London Rye, which is just coming into its own, isn't a slavish copy of any one style but brings a variety of influences to bear to create something really worthy of the London name.

Unusually, the mash bill is quite low in rye (just 42 per cent), with the balance contributed by an extra pale malt. But worry ye not, rye fans, because the lovely teasing spicy note (think nutmeg above all) that makes this grain such a joy to sip and savour is here in all its glory, alongside a delicious sweetness and some wood notes, all skilfully balanced. For such a young company it's a notable success – hats off to the distilling team. The complexity on the palate comes from a clever, if demanding, cask regime which is exactly the sort of thing that a small, pioneering distillery should be doing.

So more recently, aiming to dial up that complexity and continue to explore cask maturation and wood effects, they have collaborated with California's Sonoma Distilling Company to take the London Rye for additional maturation in a variety of casks – including ex-peated whisky barrels and Pedro Ximénez sherry casks – and also launched a Wheat whisky.

The distillery is well worth checking out. There are tours available, a great cocktail bar (the distillery makes some very fine gins) with knowledgeable and enthusiastic staff and a rather hip restaurant. So naturally, their whiskies work very well in cocktails.

I was a trifle alarmed to find on their website that they have 'beliefs'; all too often that's a symptom of folk taking themselves just a *little* too seriously. But not to worry: they lead off by standing for 'decent booze for decent prices from decent people' which in a world of lavishly packaged investment whiskies is something we can all respect and which some of their larger, longer-established and better-known counterparts north of Hadrian's Wall might do well to reflect on.

England

25

Distillery
Visitor Centre
Website

English Whisky Co.
St George's Distillery, Roudham, Norfolk
Yes
www.englishwhisky.co.uk

Whisky	
Where	
When	
Verdict	

English Whisky Co.

I took a small gamble in my first *101 Whiskies to Try Before You Die* and listed the English Whisky Company's forthcoming release from their St George's Distillery, despite the fact that it wasn't at that time legally whisky. 'This is the kind of thing that brings much-needed variety, excitement and interest to the whisky scene,' I wrote; suggesting that, 'You can buy with confidence.'

Fortunately, all turned out well and since then, the whisky coming out of the distillery has gone from strength to strength and been widely welcomed. Mind you, there were English whisky distilleries up until the early twentieth century so this is more a great tradition revived than an absolute innovation, though that hardly made things any easier for the pioneering folk at Roudham to bring English whisky to an unsuspecting world. They were the first of modern times, for which they are due much respect. Though they started in 2006, which is pretty ancient for English whisky, now just look at the number of English brands on the market, something unimaginable only a decade or so ago.

But would those Victorian drams have been as tasty and as well made as the whiskies we're getting now? I doubt it, especially if they were set against the exciting range now available from the charming St George's Distillery, where you can find anything up to ten different single-malt expressions at any one time. Naturally, with such small batch production, the choice varies over time but the distillery has now matured to the point that they can offer an 11 Year Old (likely a 12 Year Old by the time you are reading this); various wood finishes; smoky styles and, while stocks last, a handsome commemorative pack with the last bottles that will ever be signed by distillery founder Andrew Nelstrop.

I'm not sure why he's being so self-effacing because I'd be happy to admit to absolutely any of their whiskies. But permit me to draw your attention to the Original – you can probably guess where they're coming from with that one. Quite the bargain at under £40 if you shop around, it's classic in style; unpeated, matured in former bourbon casks and bottled at 43% abv to provide something archetypally English – confident, understated and well-mannered, with a steely backbone. Well done, chaps!

England

26

Distillery	**Filey Bay** Spirit of Yorkshire, Hunmanby, Yorkshire
Visitor Centre	Yes
Website	www.spiritofyorkshire.com

Whisky	
Where	
When	
Verdict	

Filey Bay

Two names crop up time and again in this book: Forsyths and Jim Swan. And here they are again, for the renowned Dr Swan consulted on the distillery's development and in its prosaic industrial home we can find two of the largest Forsyths stills outside Scotland. The wash still holds 5,000 litres and the spirit still has a 3,500-litre capacity. And they have their own four-plate column still into the bargain.

So that tells us that this is a serious, business-like operation with ambitious plans.

It's another field-to-bottle business, with joint owner Tom Mellor's farm providing the barley and handling mashing and fermentation, while the distillery itself is some two and a half miles distant and near the coastal town of Filey. Hence the Filey Bay branding and the gannet* logo embossed into the attractive bottle.

The single-minded commitment here is to whisky, so no gin or vodka (hurrah) to help with short-term finance, though the Projects releases of maturing spirit excited interest and high praise amongst those in the blogging community privileged to taste these early developments (not me: but note I'm not bitter).

But having started distilling in 2016, real whisky is available now. A range of finishes are offered, including the STR Finish (Dr Swan's hand here) alongside the Moscatel Finish and Sherry Finish and limited releases such as Yorkshire Day 2020. Bourbon casks also feature in the mix.

While field-to-bottle isn't quite the standout these days as it would have been even a few years ago, and the distillery are at pains to stress that they respect traditional practices, they haven't been afraid to innovate in a most intriguing way in the still house. While a Forsyths spirit still is familiar enough, adding the small column still to run in tandem with it is ground breaking. The aim is to produce a higher strength and sweeter spirit that allows the distiller and blender some scope for creative exploration of flavour when it comes to the final vatting.

I suppose – cliché alert – that they just had to do something different in Yorkshire. It's their spirit apparently.

England

27

Distillery	**The Lakes** The Lakes Distillery, Setmurthy, Cumbria
Visitor Centre	Yes
Website	www.lakesdistillery.com

Whisky	
Where	
When	
Verdict	

The Lakes

Another day and another new gin lands on my desk.* But that's
been the key to survival for many small distillery projects as they
wait for their whisky. Whisky's a cash-greedy business, so anything
that brings in much needed income is welcomed. Hence The
Lakes gin which, I must add, is very good. And tourism, of course.
With the bustling Lake District to boost their visitors, all wandering
lonely as a cloud and mostly too idle to actually walk up a decent
hill, bottles of The Lakes should find many a new home.

This is a relatively new operation, distilling having started in
November 2014. There was an aspiration to become England's
first whisky distillery but after some project delays they were
pipped by The English Whisky Company (see 25) and, sad to
relate, the pricing and quality of their early releases attracted some
disdainful comment. Still, there's room for all in this growing
market and The Lakes seems to sit very naturally and comfortably
in its landscape. Managing Director and founder Paul Currie has
family connections with the Arran distillery and has recruited some
serious whisky distilling talent here, led by Dhavall Gandhi –
expertise that, to judge by initial reviews, was badly needed.

But with gin and visitors keeping the cash tills ringing merrily, the
whiskies have had time and space to develop and now we're
offered an interesting range of varied expressions, styled as
Whiskymakers' Editions, alongside different cask finishes, their
own blends, such as The One, and their cask-finished proprietary
bottlings. It's an eclectic collection, though their Steel Bonnets
blend, combining both English and Scotch whisky, is perhaps little
more than a curiosity. In general, the house style tends to a sherry
finish though a glance at the impressive range suggests that they
haven't let that constrain them unduly.

The talented Mr Gandhi has been given a free hand. So too the
copywriter for the website who tells us that 'each unique bottling
is an expression of creative freedom, the product of a playground
where instinct, experience and inspiration roam free, coming
together to realise one intrinsic objective; the creation of
outstanding flavours'.

That scarcely requires any embellishment so I'll content myself
with observing that all that I have tasted have been really quite
agreeable. You could do worse than try some.

England

28

Distillery

Visitor Centre
Website

Masthouse
Copper Rivet Distillery,
Pump House no.5, Leviathan Way,
Chatham Dockyard, Kent
Yes
www.copperrivetdistillery.com

Whisky	
Where	
When	
Verdict	

DOCKYARD DISTILLED

MASTHOUSE
HANDCRAFTED
SINGLE ESTATE WHISKY

PRIDE • PROVENANCE

Green apple and
ginger biscuit,
tropical fruits and
floral mid-notes,
toasted oak,
chocolate orange
on the palate,
finished with malt
& white pepper

Variety: Belgravia
Harvest: Aug 2016
Field: 40 Acre Marsh

HEAD DISTILLER

SINGLE MALT WHISKY
Natural & unfiltered

Pot distilled in accordance with the
Invicta Whisky Charter

VINTAGE 2017

500ml

Alc 45% vol

BARREL NO:
2017/11
2017/12
2017/13
2017/14
2017/25
2017/26
2017/27
2017/28

First fill ASB &
Virgin ASB HT

RELEASED NOV 2020
BOTTLE NO:

Masthouse

I first came across the Copper Rivet Distillery when writing about their gin, but it was always their intention to release a single malt and provide us with another great example of an English single-estate whisky.

The distillery is based in the magnificent Victorian Pump House no. 5 in the historic Chatham Dockyard on the Thames Estuary, and located on the splendidly named Leviathan Way. That's quite an address but thankfully the distillery lives up to the name. It has also breathed new life into buildings which were abandoned in the mid-1980s when the dockyards were closed, something of an economic and emotional disaster for Chatham and the Medway.

Owned by the Russell family, who have links to the retail side of the drinks industry, Copper Rivet aim to reflect the engineering, innovation and entrepreneurship which once characterised this location. So, as well as buying and refurbishing the impressive building, they have worked with Master Distiller Abhi Banik, who taught at the prestigious Heriot-Watt International Centre for Brewing and Distilling in Edinburgh and, to judge by the distillery's promotional video, is something of an obsessive for quality.

So much so, in fact, that Copper Rivet have even designed their own still and (horrors!) had it built in England. The grain used for their Masthouse whiskies is specially grown Kentish malted barley from the nearby Isle of Sheppey, and the distillery take great pride in their farm-to-glass production. Following distillation, the ex-bourbon casks spend the first 12 months of their life maturing in the distillery, soaking up the Kentish climate, before spending a further two years prior to bottling.

There's a welcome commitment to transparency here, and Copper Rivet have even gone as far as writing their own Invicta Whisky Charter which sets outs the rules and standards to which the Masthouse whiskies will be made. There's lots of information on the 50-cl bottle setting out the grain variety used, the name of the field in which the grain was grown and the barrel numbers from which the spirit was taken.

Though it's still in the early stages of development, Copper Rivet has come an impressively long way. I anticipate great things to come from their dedicated and skilled team. It's definitely one to follow even if, financially, you sail before the mast.

England

29

Distillery	
Visitor Centre	
Website	

Helsinki
The Helsinki Distillery Company,
Työpajankatu 2A, Helsinki
Yes
www.hdco.fi

Whisky	
Where	
When	
Verdict	

Helsinki

The Helsinki Distilling Company is probably the smallest of the three Finnish distilleries mentioned here, but punches well above its weight and is undoubtedly the funkiest. It's located in a strikingly Brutalist brick building in a former industrial quarter of Finland's fine capital city that has, in its near-hundred-year history, served as abattoir, power plant, soap factory, meatball factory, car wash and wine cellar: if you ask me this is the best of its many lives. The area is now an achingly trendy hipster haunt with expensive designer apartments converted from shabby former industrial units – think London's Hoxton or Williamsburg in New York and you've got the idea.

But credit to founders Kai Kilpinen and Mikko Mykkänen who set up here in 2014, somewhat ahead of the curve when the local vibe was distinctly grungy, albeit with a vegan café as neighbours. They've gone on to make really good gin and a range of Finnish specialities such as Akvavit, Applejack and Lingonberry Gin Liqueur, all very tasty. The whiskeys (note the spelling) are all true small batch and four different types are made: two rye whiskeys, a single malt and even Finland's only corn whiskey, all from locally grown grains.

As well as their small distillery the guys have created a very cool tasting bar and restaurant from where they also run tours and tastings. So, in what is Helsinki's first distillery in more than a century they've provided everything you need under one roof. Except, of course, this being Finland you can't buy a bottle at the distillery. For that the locals have to trek to the government-controlled Alko chain of off-licences or take a flight somewhere and buy at the airport. The distillery will sell you your own private cask but then you have to wait at least three years to drink it!

Outside Finland, you should be able to find their 50-cl bottles in any decent online specialist. However, while it may look expensive, remember it's bottled at a tasty 47.5% abv which eases most of the sticker shock of the smaller bottle (not medicinally you understand, that's a figure of speech).

Finland

30

Distillery Kyrö
Visitor Centre Isokyrö, Finland
Website Yes
www.kyrodistillery.com

Whisky	
Where	
When	
Verdict	

Kyrö

The Kyrö Malt Rye is a relatively recent product from the team at Kyrö, better known for their multi-award-winning gin. They talk of their 'bold flavours and wild ideas' and launched this whisky with a video, perhaps influenced more than a little by Johnnie Walker's *The Man Who Walked Around the World* (starring Robert Carlyle in a tour-de-force piece of Steadicam filmmaking that will account for six and a half minutes of your life that you really have to give up). Kyrö's effort is remarkable for the heavily bearded naked man and how, in just two and a half minutes it crams in almost every known cliché about Finland and manages to plug all their products. But as they're very good and the video is quite amusing, we'll forgive them even if it subverts the comforting myth of Finns as taciturn introverts – the heavily bearded naked man is quite loquacious.

Founded as recently as 2014 by five friends in a sauna, Kyrö has gone on to considerable success backed by heavy investment that has allowed them to greatly expand production. As a result of this there should be plenty to go round and, even allowing for the fact that this comes in a smaller bottle than we're accustomed to in the UK, don't hold back as it's pretty decent value.

Finnish distilling has come a long, long way in the last decade and there are now some very impressive products emerging from the land of Lemminkäinen. This little beauty was bottled at 47.2% abv and made with 100 per cent Finnish wholegrain rye, then matured in new American oak casks. It may be hard to credit if you believe Finland to be shrouded in perpetual darkness and covered in gloomy birch forests (it is a bit though) but considerable amounts of high-quality rye and barley are grown here so a vibrant brewing and distilling industry quickly emerged with the relaxation of government regulations following full EU membership in 1995. Local taxes remain high however and a strong temperance tradition lingers on.

However, the splendidly tongue-twisting Finnish language has given us *kalsarikännit* which translates as 'to get drunk at home in your underpants with no intention of doing anything else'. You don't even need a sauna for that.

Finland

31

Distillery
Visitor Centre
Website

Teerenpeli
Teerenpeli Brewery and Distillery,
Lahti, Finland
Yes
www.teerenpeli.com

Whisky

Where

When

Verdict

Teerenpeli

Would you like to learn some more Finnish? What a great language that gives us words like *nousuhumala*, to describe the feeling of getting pleasantly drunk at the start of the evening, and *laskuhumala* for later, when you just want to fight or vomit.

And *teerenpeli*, which means 'flirtation' or 'dalliance'. Well, there is nothing flirtatious about this whisky – it is seriously well made, well packaged and well worth seeking out.

It just goes to show that whisky can continue to astonish and delight all of us. Teerenpeli have been making whisky since 2002; although initially they were only selling it at their restaurant and tiny subterranean distillery in Lahti, about 60 miles north-east of Helsinki. However, things went so well that they expanded in 2015 and now share a site with a brewery that's in the same family ownership. Annual output is more than 100,000 litres and while most of the production stays in Finland, where it has a strong local following, they have developed a modest export business on the Baltic ferries and through Helsinki airport, meaning a small quantity is starting to leave the warehouses for us to enjoy.

As a result supplies of their Aged 10 Years single malt or the cheeky Kaski are beginning to enjoy international distribution and should be found in better specialists (you can always ask your favourite supplier to stock it). They have a peaty variant, known as Savu, and the more recently introduced Kulo which has spent seven years in sherry casks and is bottled at over 50% abv. This is a rich and full-flavoured tribute to the impact of quality wood and using oloroso and Pedro Ximénez sherry casks. In particular, the PX sherry has contributed a splendid note of raisin sweetness.

You can visit the distillery and associated brewery and eat well at the restaurant. As I've been banging on about them for nearly a decade now, I was delighted that Teerenpeli was named Worldwide Whiskey Producer 2020 by the influential International Wine & Spirit Competition. It's a fantastic, fully justified accolade for a small distiller in a remote location in a country not historically associated with whisky – against a shortlist including such renowned operations as Kavalan and Sazerac of the USA. It should be on your shortlist too.

32

Distillery

Visitor Centre

Website

Eddu
Distillerie des Menhirs, Plomelin, Brittany
Yes
www.distillerie.bzh

Whisky	
Where	
When	
Verdict	

WHISKY PUR BLÉ NOIR

EDDU

BROCÉLIANDE

WHISKY DE BRETAGNE
Vieilli en fût de Chêne de France

DISTILLERIE
DES MENHIRS

Eddu

Apart from the very obvious big thing about this distillery – what you might call the 800-kilo standing stone in the room – there is something else curious, different and very French about how whisky is made at the Distillerie des Menhirs.

It's the addition of demineralised spring water to the barrels of maturing spirit as they age, gradually reducing the strength to prepare it for bottling. It's a practice widely seen in Cognac and Armagnac but not, as far as I am aware, employed for whisky anywhere outside of France.

But what's even more unusual and distinctive is their decision, virtually unique, to distil using buckwheat. In fact, when the Eddu brand (meaning 'buckwheat' in the local Breton language) was launched in 1998 it was the world's first buckwheat whisky and remained so until their pioneering work was emulated by several small distillers in the USA. For the pedantic amongst us, buckwheat isn't technically a grain ('the seed or fruit of a cereal grass') so arguably this isn't whisky. However, in the spirit of *liberté, égalité et fraternité* we'll let that pass.

The Distillerie des Menhirs, which remains in the founding Le Lay family, traces its history to 1921 when a second-hand mobile still was purchased to make lambig. That's a type of apple brandy, not dissimilar to Calvados, though that is made in Normandy and here we're in Brittany – home to Asterix the Gaul and the land of menhirs (the giant standing stones). In 1996, after some innovations in lambig, Guy Le Lay turned to the possibilities of buckwheat, once an important food crop but by then somewhat neglected. It proved challenging to distil, but persistence with the distillery's unique direct-fired stills (their design drawn from both Scotland and Cognac), and the use of very high-quality French oak barrels and the phased reduction of the strength of the spirit, resulted in the launch of the first Eddu Silver style in 2002.

Today the range has grown to include expressions at 5, 10 and even 15 years of age and Eddu Grey Rock, a barley and buckwheat whisky. The premium Eddu Brocéliande spends five years in French Limousin oak barrels, with finishing in new oak barrels from the Brocéliande forest.

France

33

Distillery | **Glann ar Mor**
Visitor Centre | Glann ar Mor, Pleubian, Brittany
Website | Yes
| www.glannarmor.com

Whisky	
Where	
When	
Verdict	

CELTIC WHISKY DISTILLERIE

Kornog

WHISKY SINGLE MALT TOURBÉ

Né par le feu, élevé par le vent

70cl   PRODUIT DE FRANCE   46%vol

Glann ar Mor

Amongst the pioneers of the early French whisky industry based in Brittany is the Glann ar Mor distillery of Jean and Martine Donnay, who by 2005 had established this small and very traditional operation. It is characterised by a strict adherence to old-school practices such as wooden washbacks; direct firing of the stills; external worm-tub condensers and bottling at 46% abv or higher without chill filtration or added caramel colour. All of which are familiar enough on today's craft-distilling landscape but represented something of a consciously nostalgic, almost deliberately retrograde, approach when the distillery was established, defying the industry norms of the day. Islay whiskies in particular appear to have been a particular inspiration, alongside an affinity between Gaelic and Breton culture.

Glann ar Mor means 'by the seaside' in Breton, and great stress is laid by the distillery on their location right on Brittany's northern coast where they maintain the microclimate adds a maritime note to the whisky and aids a relatively fast rate of maturation. Presumably with that in mind, Jean Donnay has long proposed a distillery on Islay at Gartbreck. Though planning permission has been granted this has yet to come to fruition and the project has been marked by various arcane disputes with putative partners.

Though historically output has been quite limited there are two principal expressions: Glann ar Mor (unpeated) and the peated Kornog (or 'west wind'), available as Roc'hir, in a 12 Years Old version and on occasion as cask strength or varied cask finishes. Both have attracted praise from enthusiasts, Kornog in particular. A 100 per cent rye variant – the aptly named Only Rye – was also released. Though this is not currently available, most of the expressions including the limited editions are offered through their online retail operation Tregor Whisky (but check first if they are able to ship to your location).

In June 2020 it was announced that the Donnays had sold their business to Maison Villevert, a longstanding spirits producer in Cognac with expertise in distillation, brand creation and marketing. At the present time, their plans for Glann ar Mor remain unclear though as their first step into whisky there will doubtless be further developments. The future plans of Jean and Martine have also yet to be revealed but will surely be noteworthy, exciting and well worth following, on Islay or their native shore.

34

Distillery	**Warenghem**
	Distillerie Warenghem, Lannion, Brittany
Visitor Centre	Yes
Website	www.distillerie-warenghem.bzh

Whisky	
Where	
When	
Verdict	

Warenghem

One of the great things about making whisky outside the established nations is that you are free from the cultural reference points that both define and constrain your work. Consider distillery architecture. It has taken The Macallan to break free of the pagoda cliché that bedevils Scottish distilleries, even brand-new ones. Though almost entirely redundant they still appear on the landscape and it has taken a 'luxury brand' (sigh) to develop some fresh design language for the semiotics of a distillery's home.

So it's quite fitting that the Warenghem distillery, the first to distil whisky in France, has challenged that orthodoxy with its boldly cantilevered first-floor tasting room soaring out towards the Léguer valley. It's simply stunning. Warenghem was established in 1900 to make liqueurs but pioneered French whisky in 1987, graduating to single malt by 1998. Today, under their Armorik, Breizh, Galleg, WB and Yeun Elez (the 'Gateway to Hell' apparently) brands they offer both blended and single malt styles in a variety of expressions, which they proudly style 'Breton Whisky' – the rugged Brittany countryside considers itself a Celtic nation and a vigorous cultural and political nationalist movement thrives here.

While Scotland may have provided the initial inspiration, in the context of Brittany's cultural and linguistic links to other Celtic communities, the distillation of whisky makes perfect sense as an expression of national or regional identity and Warenghem feels distinctly both French and Breton.

Yet this is whisky as Scots writers from Robert Burns, Aeneas MacDonald* to Neil Gunn would recognise it, imbued with a deeper metaphorical significance and meaning than a mere drink. In the face of such profound considerations, today's talk of whisky as a financial investment is revealed as callow and tawdry. Producers such as this remind us of whisky's artisanal roots and its spiritual significance. Not for nothing has the French government declared them the first French whisky distillery to be an *Entreprise du Patrimoine Vivant*. Even if their whisky is hard to find, true whisky lovers should salute them.

France

---

* Did you know Aeneas MacDonald's real name was George Malcolm Thomson? The first writer on whisky from the standpoint of the consumer, he adopted a pseudonym in order not to offend his teetotaller mother.

35

Distillery Blaue Maus, Eggolsheim-Neuses
Visitor Centre Yes
Website www.fleischmann-whisky.de

Blaue Maus

Whisky	
Where	
When	
Verdict	

Blaue Maus

This is Germany's oldest single-malt whisky distillery and there are many more besides. In fact, today more than 60 distilleries are now making German whisky. Yes, 60 – though some reports claim it's more than 150, with an Association of German Whisky Distillers (Verband Deutscher Whiskybrenner VDW) who have a whisky trail and promote German Whisky Day on the last Saturday of June every year.

It's clear that Germany has taken to whisky with some enthusiasm which, given the country's long distilling tradition, should come as no surprise. Of course, most of these operations are very, very small; their production is extremely limited and, as they have a wealthy domestic market with some of the most enthusiastic and well-informed consumers on the planet, very little German whisky actually leaves the country.

But Fleischmann's Blaue Maus distillery is the original and genuine article so worthy of our attention even if rarer than the eponymous rodent from which it takes its name.

Its origins can be traced to 1983 but the owners weren't satisfied with the quality and nothing appeared on the open market until Glen Mouse (now Blaue Maus) was released in 1986. From there, following expansion in 2012, their range has exploded to include the Green Dog, Black Pirate, the unusual Stacking Bottle – which consists of three different 20-cl bottles of your choice – and many more besides. There is even the Sylter Tide Whisky where the casks were floated in the North Sea and which comes in a bottle immersed beneath the waves until overgrown with barnacles. Try getting that past the Scotch Whisky Association as a maturation technique!

Apparently, nearly 40 years ago at the start of operations, no one told the then owner Robert Fleischmann that he should char the inside of the barrels, so it never occurred to him to do so, going on to form part of the distillery's distinctive and idiosyncratic style.

Experimentation, innovation and a sense of mischief – what's not to like? Along with up to 149 others, Blaue Maus should make us think again about what whisky is and could be. On second thoughts, I might draw the line at maturing whisky in the sea but. . . well, whatever floats your boat I suppose.

Germany

36

Distillery
Visitor Centre
Website

Finch
Finch Distillery, Heroldstatt, Swabia
Yes
www.finch-whisky.com

Whisky	
Where	
When	
Verdict	

Finch

Located high in the Swabian Alps, a picturesque but sparsely populated part of south-west Germany, we find the Finch Distillery of farmer and distillery owner Hans-Gerhard Fink. Small-scale distillation began here in 1999 but today, though the products are not widely distributed outside of Germany, it is one of the country's largest whisky producers, with an annual production of some 250,000 litres, equivalent to around 400,000 bottles even after maturation. They also have one of Germany's largest pot stills, some 3,000-litres capacity and of unique design, linked to a downstream column. This was installed in 2012, after which production was stepped up and subsequently expanded to include gin (including a licence for the *Playboy* brand), vodka and traditional German fruit brandies.

Thanks to Herr Fink's ownership of around a thousand acres of farmland growing barley, wheat, spelt and emmer (an early wheat variety forming the main cereal grain of the Bronze and Iron Age) this is a true field-to-bottle operation, the distillery maintaining that this gives them a high degree of quality control through every stage of the process.

So though Finch may have started as a hobby, today it is a serious professional operation with Finch Adventure World, a substantial visitor experience under development to add to the existing distillery tours and tastings.

There are a number of Swabian Highland Whisky expressions including the Private Edition Single Cask 10 Years; Madeira, sherry, Islay cask, red wine barrique and finishes, alongside corn, rye and Dinkel Port-finish whiskies. A tribute to the diverse cereal production possible here, this latter is distilled from the farm's own spelt grain (*dinkel*), then matured for eight years in port casks. It is far from a run-of-the-mill style and a further demonstration of the innovation and creativity found in the new producing nations.

Despite the scale, bottling is still essentially a manual operation with a small hand-filling line and application of the distinctive wire closures. There is no chill filtration and strictly no added colour, the German whisky consumer being particularly sensitive to the addition of spirit caramel (E150a, indicated by the wording '*Mit Farbstoff*' and particularly dreaded by the cognoscenti).

Also, hier ist es nicht bekannt!

Germany

37

Distillery Slyrs, Schliersee-Neuhaus
Visitor Centre Yes
Website www.slyrs.de

Slyrs

Whisky	
Where	
When	
Verdict	

Slyrs

Originally known as Lantenhammer, like so many new whisky distilleries, when this was first opened in 1928 it was to make brandy and fruit spirits. Whisky's new-found fashionability and a trip to Scotland persuaded the Master Distiller to try producing whisky in 1999, making Slyrs one of the founding fathers of European whisky and, as they proudly maintain, the first in Bavaria. By 2007, and under new management, it was enough of a success for them to install their own custom-designed pot stills, and further expansion in 2009 and 2010 means that this is not exactly a boutique operation any more.

Their whisky is highly regarded and has performed well in blind tasting against some top-class competition. With releases such as their splendid Rye, Slyrs might even give one or two very well-established names a fright. Mind you, Scotland can't compete with the Mountain Edition, which is matured in the distillery's unique high-altitude warehouse some 1,501 metres above sea level. To better that, someone would have to build a 150-metre-high platform on the summit of Ben Nevis with a warehouse on top. That's just silly.

Distribution beyond Germany is, as ever, limited but the influential online retailer Master of Malt have built a relationship with Slyrs which means they have several high-strength single-cask releases, and their sister business That Boutique-y Whisky Company offers a 3-year-old Slyrs bottling.

Back at the distillery tourism is clearly important, with the possibility to select a self-guided visit, a guided tour or a masterclass. Or, for a really hands-on experience, you can book a workshop and try creating your own Slyrs whisky liqueur.

Then there is the option of a Private Cask programme. This starts at close to €4,000 for the 40-litre option and runs to over €13,500 for a 110-litre cask if, as I did out of curiosity, you click on a few options. I'd suggest this was the BMW of German whiskies but we seem to be getting into Maybach territory here. Fortunately for Mrs B's piece of mind I resisted pushing the final 'buy' button and thanks to That Boutique-y Whisky Company we can start with a cheeky little VW.

Germany

38

Distillery
Visitor Centre
Website

Flóki
Eimwerk Distillery, Gardabaer
No – visits by appointment
www.flokiwhisky.is

Whisky

Where

When

Verdict

Flóki

By now you'll be in little doubt that whisky has conquered the world – even far-flung corners such as Gardabaer (no, I haven't any idea either but apparently it's near Reykjavík) where Iceland's first, and currently only, drams are distilled. The distillery itself resembles a large Nissen hut but inside there's the reassuring sight of a Holstein pot still capable of producing around 100,000 litres of spirit annually. To be fair, around half of this is reserved for gin and aquavit but that should still leave enough whisky for Iceland's 341,243 inhabitants to enjoy, if it wasn't for the fact that the entrepreneurial owners have achieved notable export success.

This is a family operation, founded as long ago as 2009, though it took four years and apparently 163 trial distillations and maturation tests to ensure the perfect recipe, so the first single-malt whisky wasn't available until 2017 (though the 2-year-old Young Malt range dates from 2014). Since then there has been a steady flow of new expressions, all using 100 per cent Icelandic barley sourced from just three local farms – who also, presumably, provide the sheep droppings over which some of it is dried. That may sound strange but it's a traditional Icelandic method of preserving food and heating houses.

Maturation is in new American oak casks, leading the distillery to suggest that what results is 'a complex malt with a unique blend of characteristics found in Bourbon, Scotch, and Irish whiskies'. There are a range of finishes, including the Sheep Dung Smoked, as well as the Sherry Cask and Beer Barrel and a highly unusual expression finished for three months in Icelandic birch wood casks – any longer and the losses would be too great as birch is more porous than oak.

The name Flóki is derived from the Viking explorer Hrafna-Flóki who, guided by three ravens (an early form of sat-nav), discovered Iceland in 868 and is the first recorded inhabitant. Interestingly, Eimwerk is not the island's only distillery. William Grant & Sons make their Reyka vodka here and there are other smaller operations producing fruit and birch-based spirit and other specialities catering to the local and tourism markets. However, without making too great a saga out of it, let's salute Flóki's pioneering approach and innovative attitude.

Iceland

39

Distillery Amrut
Visitor Centre Amrut, Bangalore
Website Yes
www.amrutdistilleries.com

Whisky

Where

When

Verdict

AMRUT
fusion
SINGLE MALT WHISKY

DISTILLERS FOR OVER THREE GENERATIONS

70cl ℮ / 700 ml ℮ | 50% alc./vol.

DISTILLED, MATURED AND BOTTLED BY
AMRUT DISTILLERIES PVT. LTD.
(N.R. JAGDALE GROUP)
KAMBIPURA, BENGALURU-560074, INDIA
PRODUCT OF INDIA

BENGALURU INDIA

Amrut

2004 isn't so very long ago. Yet the world of whisky was so different then that Amrut Distilleries' UK launch of their single malt in August of that year – in Glasgow of all places – was largely greeted with indifference, or met rank disbelief that good-quality whisky could be made in India.

However, blind testing amongst consumers – even in Scotland – had shown positive results, with drinkers comparing it to a Speyside single malt, so Amrut determined to persist. As their current boss remarked, 'We thought if our product had to pass the test, why not do so in the toughest location. Scotland is the home of Scotch. If they acknowledge our single malt, then that's good enough for me.'

And in the end so it proved. Early reviews and high scores from leading magazines turned the tide, and Indian single malt now enjoys a position of respect in world markets, with the family-owned Amrut noted for its quality and innovation. It's all the more impressive when you consider that the company was founded as recently as 1948 and their single-malt expressions are made in a distillery built in 1987.

Amrut make lots of different limited-edition expressions including their Double Cask;, Naarangi; Madeira Finish, Greedy Angels (in various styles), Two Continents, Herald, Rye and a Port Pipe Peated.That, frankly, sounds horrid – I can't imagine two flavour influences less suited to each other. Some are now hard to find and some, such as the Greedy Angels Peated Rum 10 Years Old cask expression, quite extraordinarily expensive – it's £800 on one leading website. But there's no need to spend a lot of money to enjoy something distinctive and high quality, with an unusually pronounced flavour, that, once tasted, you won't forget in a hurry.

Fusion, pretty much their UK flagship product, is such a whisky, unique in combining Indian barley from the Himalayas with peated malt from Scotland, and bottled without chill filtration at a healthy 50% abv. And, despite that, and despite having come halfway round the world, it's excellent value, typically available for just under £50.

So it seems that 2004 is a very long time ago indeed. The past may well be a foreign country but, as far as whisky is concerned, this particular country is very much part of its present and its future.

India

40

Distillery

Visitor Centre
Website

Paul John
Paul John Distillery, Cuncolim,
South Goa
Yes
www.jdl.in

Whisky	
Where	
When	
Verdict	

Paul John

No longer a surprise or a novelty, Indian whisky is now a true global force, fully meriting this second, and indeed a third, entry. The company behind Paul John is a relatively new one, founded only in 1996 but growing rapidly in both home and export markets. In October 2012, they first launched their whiskies in the UK and, like the other Indian distillers featured here, they have been refreshingly bold and innovative in experimenting with a wide range of competitively priced finishes and alternative styles.

In fact, their 'entry level' expression Nirvana is currently less than £30, which seems uncommon value for something they once described as offering 'sublime experiences beyond the worldly realm'. But, back here on Planet Earth, I'd spend a few pounds more and trade up to the slightly higher strength Brilliance. It's a bold name to put on any whisky but the company themselves suggest that they are 'driven by the zest to break conventions, [and] . . . set out to penetrate the highest strata of the world of whisky'. Considering such vaunting ambition it seems churlish to forgo a few extra pennies (well, a tenner to be precise). Trust me, you'll be happy you did and as the packaging is well up to Western standards you can safely present the bottle to those few of your more snobbish whisky friends who have yet to receive the memo about Indian whisky.

While this doesn't carry an age statement, and is definitely young by Scottish standards, the taste belies its youth; the maturation conditions of Asian whiskies (think also of Taiwan) are such that old-world considerations simply don't apply. We can't reliably judge these whiskies against the long-established norms that apply to colder northern climes. Master Distiller Michael D'Souza notes that: 'Whisky matured at these temperatures simply cannot be aged for the kind of time expected with Scotch, even trying to mature our whisky for just 10 years would leave barely a bottle of liquid in the barrel'. But frankly, Indian whiskies such as these have long gone past the point of comparison with Scotch, or any other whisky, and stand purely and proudly on their own.

With Goa popular with tourists, a visitor centre was opened in November 2018 at the Cuncolim distillery. Here they offer tastings or the option of a full-day tour, from mashing to distilling, and culminating in a visit to the underground cellars.

India

41

Distillery

Visitor Centre
Website

Rampur
Rampur Distillery, Rampur,
Uttar Pradesh
No – visits by appointment
www.rampursinglemalt.com

Whisky	
Where	
When	
Verdict	

Rampur

What's the best-selling whisky in the world? If you guessed Johnnie Walker you'd be wrong. In fact, it's the little-known Officer's Choice, which outsells Walker roughly two to one. Of course, 'little-known' is quite incorrect. As its staggering sales demonstrate – Officer's Choice alone sells over 32 million cases annually – it's very well known indeed at home, which just happens to be India. Even Rampur's 8PM brand, which is well down the Indian bestselling list, racks up rather more than seven million cases which would make it comfortably the world's third-largest-selling Scotch.

Rampur, based in the foothills of the Himalayas and one of India's oldest distilleries, currently offers their Select single-malt expression with a Double Cask and PX Sherry Finish as well. Double Cask is an excellent product. 'Rather nice' is how one understated Scots distiller described it. But then, this is a serious distilling operation – one of the largest in Asia. They've recently made some substantial investments in new distilling and climate and humidity-controlled warehouse facilities, indicative of the serious long-term thinking behind their single malts and the company's commitment to quality.

No surprise, then, that Rampur has been looking at the lucrative European markets with interest and employing Scottish expertise to provide the essential skills. The legendary Dr Jim Swan was involved in their early single-malt production and, more recently, former Diageo Master Distiller Charlie Smith (once of Talisker and latterly responsible for getting Ballindalloch up and running) has been working to install new distilling plant capable of producing 2 million litres of spirit annually.

Don't ignore the great value to be found in Select and Double Cask, but I'd point you towards their most recent release, Asava for something that has nicely integrated a nod to old-world single-malt tradition with a touch of distinctively Indian heritage. Though no age statement is shown, Asava has been matured in American bourbon barrels for around two-thirds of its life, then finished in Indian Cabernet Sauvignon casks (there's been wine made in India since the Bronze Age though not much finds its way out of the country). At 45% abv and non-chill filtered, this is more than 'rather nice'.

India

42

Distillery Blackwater
Visitor Centre Yes
Website www.blackwaterdistillery.ie

Blackwater
Blackwater, Ballyduff, County Kerry

Whisky	
Where	
When	
Verdict	

Blackwater

Until very recently, virtually all Irish whiskey came from one of three very large distilleries, so whatever the label implied – and some operators were economical with the strict truth – independent bottlers and newbie distillers desperate for some cash flow and brand awareness had little choice. Until 2014 there was no equivalent of the Scotch Whisky Association to police the market but, following the establishment of the Irish Whiskey Association (now Drinks Ireland), a Technical File covering the production of Irish whiskey was adopted into EU law.

That, you would imagine, has to be a good thing. Well, there's an old proverb, 'He who pays the piper calls the tune', and, according to some of the new generation of Irish distillers, that was primarily the Pernod Ricard subsidiary, Irish Distillers Ltd (largest of the Big Three). The Technical File determines that: 'Irish Pot Still Whiskey must be made from a mash which contains a minimum of 30% malted barley and a minimum of 30% unmalted barley, with up to 5% of other cereals such as oats and rye added if required.' Which just happens to suit the big boys.

Enter Peter Mulryan, broadcaster, whisky author and CEO of the Blackwater Distillery. He has been digging through historical records going back several hundred years and maintains that other cereals were certainly used at up to 20 per cent of the mash bill and possibly considerably more.

Does this matter? Well, Blackwater and a number of other new distilleries want to innovate, to experiment, to recreate historical styles and generally stretch the possibilities of cereal in a pot still. That's their risk, of course, but exciting for curious drinkers.

So Blackwater, first established in 2014 but distilling in Ballyduff since 2018, are now making what they claim to be 'the kind of Single Pot Still whisky Ireland was once famous for, and not the neutered, revisionist spirit that has hijacked the name'.

And what does it taste like? Well, I can't say because their whisky (their preferred spelling), described as Single Malt and Heritage Pot Still Irish in 'the old-fashioned way . . . made with 100% Irish barley, oats, wheat and rye', won't be ready until early 2022.

Come the day of the launch I expect some fireworks.

P.S. Our mystery bottle is because Blackwater's design was still top secret as we went to print.

Ireland

43

Distillery | **Clonakilty**
Visitor Centre | Clonakilty, Clonakilty, Co. Cork
Website | Yes
| www.clonakiltydistillery.ie

Whisky

Where

When

Verdict

Clonakilty

As a further representative of the incredible expansion of Irish distilling that has boomed in recent years, I give you Clonakilty, a €10 million project in the eponymous coastal town in the south of Ireland. It was the creation of a local farming family, the Scullys, backed by a small group of private investors. The Scullys have worked the land here for nine generations and will be providing the heritage barley varieties for the pot still varieties. Not being distillers by trade, they hired Paul Corbett, after his two years at Teeling Distillery in Dublin, as Head Distiller. He took charge of their three pot stills in the dramatic glass-clad still house with its potential to produce around 500,000 litres annually. That's significant by craft-distilling standards but modest when compared to the Irish giants, though Clonakilty will clearly have ambitions beyond their home.

All production is then warehoused in a new facility on the Galley Head peninsula overlooking the Atlantic Ocean where the distillery suggest it will absorb the 'ocean infused' salty air (while that might be a bit of a marketing myth it seems to work for Bruichladdich, Talisker and others).

The initial releases under the Clonakilty brand are all third-party bottlings, finished to Clonakilty's specifications. In addition, they have an interesting range of 'Partnership' expressions where they have worked with various US craft breweries to finish whiskey in former beer casks. Unlike a number of their competitors, the website makes it quite clear that these whiskeys weren't distilled by Clonakilty. They are all Irish of course and while the original source remains obscure the well-informed among you can probably hazard a decent guess as to their genesis.

But looking to the future, the distillery's new make has attracted some praise. As the first Clonakilty distilled whiskey should be available shortly after this book reaches the shelves, and as this is evidently a serious operation, I'm going to jump right in with the thought that it will be one to seek out.

Finally, and I'll freely admit quite irrelevantly, I like this distillery because they support conservation work for whales and dolphins and put a whale's tail on their label. Who doesn't like whales? I know I do.

Ireland

44

Distillery
Visitor Centre
Website

Dingle
The Dingle Whiskey Distillery, Dingle,
County Kerry
Yes
www.dingledistillery.ie

Whisky	
Where	
When	
Verdict	

Dingle

Back in December 2012, Dingle was amongst the very first of the new wave of smaller Irish distilleries to begin operations, and their first public release of whiskey came in late 2016. There are two types of whiskey produced here: single malt and pot still, all from three splendid traditional pot stills from the renowned Forsyths. All this now takes place under the experienced eye of Master Distiller Graham Coull, also from Scotland and a veteran of the industry with experience at both William Grant's Speyside distilleries and the nearby Glen Moray, where he spent 14 years.

Stepping back in time, Dingle was founded by three craft-brewing entrepreneurs – Oliver Hughes, Liam LaHart and Peter Mosley – who anticipated a revival of small-scale distilling to echo the development of craft beers.

Backed by a crowdfunding exercise in which 500 Founding Fathers purchased a cask, the distillery remains in private ownership and today the contribution of the Fathers' fantastic foresight is recognised in the limited release of just 500 bottles of a cask-strength version of each batch of new whiskey. The distillery also continues to offer a limited cask purchase opportunity, the Descendants programme, with prices from €10,000 before excise duty and VAT.

Thankfully, though production remains at a modest four casks a day, a single bottle is rather more attainable and recent releases have been creatively exploring the effect of different cask finishes, including oloroso, Pedro Ximénez and Madeira casks alongside the more conventional ex-bourbon. Different batches of both the pot still and single malt will offer alternative approaches to finishing, which will be reflected in an evolving taste profile – read the description carefully if you favour a particular flavour in your whiskey.

Given that the company will shortly enter its second decade, making it a veteran of the Irish whiskey revival, I'm encouraged that it has remained independent and delighted to read this on their website: 'The Dingle Whiskey Distillery is not in the business of creating megabrands, nor do we distil for anyone else. Our scale is modest, our approach to what we make is essentially artisan and we have rekindled the tradition of independent distilling in Ireland.' Amen to that, I say.

Ireland

45

Distillery Kilbeggan
Visitor Centre Kilbeggan, Kilbeggan, Westmeath
Website Yes
www.kilbegganwhiskey.com

Whisky	
Where	
When	
Verdict	

Kilbeggan

There isn't room here to even begin to explain the vagaries of the Irish whiskey industry and its changing fortunes. Whole books have been written about this but Kilbeggan's history offers some of the story in microcosm. Founded in 1757, it's been bought and sold, opened, closed and then reopened, suffered from fire and Prohibition, been the subject of lawsuits and political scandal and continually changed its name.

John Teeling, then owner of the Cooley Distillery, acquired the Kilbeggan Distillery in 1987 after the building had been saved by a community trust. By 2007 he had the old place working again, though it remained somewhat ramshackle in appearance. Beam Inc of the USA took it over in December 2011 but were themselves acquired by Suntory in April 2014. Ever the entrepreneur, John Teeling moved on to found the Great Northern Distillery in Dundalk, while his sons opened their own distillery in Dublin as Teeling (see 46). Did I mention it gets confusing?

At least today there is some stability under Beam Suntory, their deep pockets and global reach giving Kilbeggan the stable future its long history deserves. And there are some interesting whiskeys being produced here (though not the misleadingly named Kilbeggan Single Grain, which is made at Kilbeggan's sister, Cooley). Confused yet?

Notable amongst these Kilbeggan-made whiskeys are the Small Batch Rye and the more recent Single Pot Still, which unusually includes a modest percentage of oats in the mash bill and claims to be distilled in the oldest working whiskey pot still in the world. This is indeed impressive, but perhaps less so when you learn that it came out of the original Tullamore distillery. A new Tullamore distillery has been built and is today owned by William Grant & Sons, the people behind Glenfiddich. Told you it was confusing!

But, if you're still with me, here's the good news: this storied old distillery is working again, actually making this whiskey which is thankfully sold at a sensible price. So you can drink deeply to Irish whiskey's tortuous history and tangled past and its rather more glowing future prospects. As an introduction to a great distilling nation you could do worse, even if today it's controlled from other islands far, far away.

Ireland

Distillery Teeling, Newmarket, Dublin
Visitor Centre Yes
Website www.teelingwhiskey.com

Whisky

Where

When

Verdict

Teeling

I have absolutely no idea at all what my ancestors were doing in 1782. I'm not sure that I care. In fact, perhaps it's better that I don't know.

However, if we study our family trees, as Jack and Stephen Teeling have done, sometimes we find much to learn and to encourage us. In their case, working back to 1782 they found something interesting: their forefather Walter Teeling, and later his son John, were distillers. Better still, they were Dublin distillers; one of 30 or so in The Liberties, then a vibrant part of Dublin and in the late-eighteenth century arguably the distilling capital of the world, as it would remain for many years afterwards. That makes them, at least in a modest way, distilling aristocracy. As far as heritage goes it doesn't get much better.

How wonderful then that his descendants have been able to establish their distillery within a few yards of where their forefather set up his stills, though that operation seems to have been quickly absorbed into a larger concern in the nearby – and splendidly named – Marrowbone Lane.

However, the Teelings reappeared in distilling's history in 1987 when their father John established Cooley Distillery. Brothers Jack and Stephen worked for the family concern until shortly after its 2012 acquisition by Beam Inc. There was no falling out; simply a recognition that their entrepreneurial spirit would never sit entirely comfortably in a corporate structure. Control from Deerfield, Illinois simply didn't appeal.

Once run-down and neglected, The Liberties is now seriously hip so it's the natural, right and fitting home for the Teeling brothers to build their distillery – the first new distillery in Dublin in 125 years, though others have since followed.

Starting with some shrewdly selected third-party bottlings, the distillery is now on stream and offers a considerable range of their own whiskeys, including Single Grain, Single Pot Still, Single Malt, Small Batch and the mighty Brabazon bottlings (though I'm not sure if I'd have named my whiskey after a bold but failed airliner).*

Teeling have taken a bold approach to product development and, with their previous experience and significant production expertise, have adopted a very reasonable pricing policy to attract new customers to their brand and lively visitor centre.

Ireland

---

* The mighty Bristol Brabazon, designed for ultra-luxurious trans-Atlantic travel. The project was abandoned in 1953 as commercially unviable.

47

Distillery

Visitor Centre
Website

Waterford
Waterford Distillery, Grattan Quay,
Waterford
No – visits by appointment
www.waterfordwhisky.com

Whisky	
Where	
When	
Verdict	

WATERFORD

IRISH SINGLE MALT WHISKY

SINGLE FARM ORIGIN

BALLYMORGAN
EDITION 1.2

DISTILLED AT WATERFORD DISTILLERY
PRODUCE OF IRELAND

Waterford

'We're embarking on a long journey, as ambitious as it's pioneering . . . to create not just the most compelling Irish whisky, but the world's most profound single malt.'

Well, that's ambitious. The thing is, the main man here has a track record that instantly recommends him to single-malt enthusiasts. And a style that offends the panjandrums of the whisky establishment. Meet Mark Reynier, iconoclast, innovator, disruptor and the man who, virtually single-handedly, dragged Islay's Bruichladdich back into noisy, irreverent life.

After that company was acquired by Remy Cointreau, Mark moved on. But not to play golf or sail his yacht but to reinvent himself whilst challenging the whisky orthodoxy which holds that *terroir* – the impact of the natural environment including soil, topography, climate and, above all, barley variety – has little or no impact on whisky's final flavour. With his background in the wine industry, Mark disagrees. Loudly.

So in 2015, backed by many of his previous investors, he bought a former brewery in Waterford, converting its state-of-the-art equipment into a distillery to produce whiskies demonstrating his theories.

If you were producing a best-selling blended whisky there are probably more important considerations than tracking provenance back to the farm that grew the barley. Fair enough: but this is far from a best-selling blend.

The distillery is home to a 'cathedral of malt' where barley grown on 19 distinct soil types on 86 different Irish farms, including organic and biodynamic, is stored. Using a custom-designed digital logistics system to keep track, each farmer's crop is harvested, stored, malted and distilled separately, aiming to capture in spirit each farm's *téireoir*, that subtle character shaped by microclimate and soil. Don't you just love the cultural appropriation in the linguistic mutation of *terroir*?

So there are lots of expressions and, as Waterford gets into its stride, there will be many more – all different, some in subtle ways and some very marked. Having tried several, I'm a believer and checking the *téireoir* code on every carton allows purchasers to pore over maps, details of the harvest, grower and distillation as well as view the full spectrum of the casks. Paradise, in fact, for whisky geeks and vindication of one man's obsession. Oh, and he's recently built a rum distillery on Grenada.

Ireland

48

Distillery
Visitor Centre
Website

West Cork
West Cork, Skibbereen,
County Cork
Yes
www.westcorkdistillers.com

Whisky

Where

When

Verdict

West Cork

With a production capacity of 4.5 million litres of whiskey and stills for gin as well, I'd have to acknowledge that West Cork is on the large side. But quite a lot of production seems to go for private label and, as the company was established in 2003 in the back room of someone's house (which sounds just the teeniest bit like, you know, that poitín stuff – my lawyer says I must stress that this is a joke and only an opinion, though you have to wonder*. . .), it feels like a tale of cask-strength success so we'll stretch a point. And, anyway, their recent expansion and return to private ownership was backed by the Irish government's Strategic Investment Fund so everything is tickety-boo.

It's a real rags-to-riches story and, with this part of Ireland not long on local employment opportunities, great news for the community as well as the founders. When John O'Connell, Ger McCarthy and Denis McCarthy first set up their suspiciously small stills (just joking, lads) it made very little economic sense to do so, so it's great to salute their pioneering spirit. That included the Rocket, a hand-built still, reputedly then the fastest in the world. Investment from the UK's Halewood Group followed and by 2014 the operation moved to Market Street in Skibbereen. Quite admirably, their stated aim is to make Irish whiskey accessible while maintaining Irish ownership. That's where the Irish taxpayer came in, stepping up in September 2019 with €18 million to buy out Halewood.

Today they operate on a 12.5-acre site where a tremendous range of expressions are produced. A visitor centre to showcase the West Cork heritage is under development and should have opened by the time you read this. So what about the whiskeys? Right now the expressions are many and varied, including a considerable number of unusual cask finishes, all in a very handsome presentation. And keep their desire to be 'accessible' in mind because, as well as very reasonable-looking retail pricing, with their Whiskey Cask Club they also have what looks like one of the best private cask purchase deals I've seen in some time.

Ireland

49

Distillery
Visitor Centre
Website

Milk & Honey
The M&H Distillery, Tel-Aviv
Yes
www.mh-distillery.com

Whisky	
Where	
When	
Verdict	

Milk & Honey

Once again we encounter the work of the indefatigable Dr Jim Swan, who played a huge role in the early development of this Israeli distillery (which to their credit they acknowledge very fully).

Putting a distillery in the heart of Tel-Aviv where summer temperatures regularly reach 30 °C and heatwaves can see the thermometer hit a toasty 40 °C might not, on the face of it, seem a terribly clever idea. But if Dr Jim was known for anything it was for mastering the art of whisky distilling and cask management in unpromising surroundings, so when the founders decided to press ahead with Israel's first whisky distillery they turned to the right man for advice. And just as well for, right from the start, Milk & Honey saw themselves on an international stage with a production capacity of up to 800,000 litres a year. So they don't lack ambition.

And, they have definitely had something of an impact because subsequently another three Israeli distilleries have begun making whisky. But to the pioneers at Milk & Honey goes the credit for blazing this trail and, as they've been producing now since 2015, they are able to present quite a range as well as offering the opportunity to buy your own private cask.

The Jim Swan signature STR casks appear in their Classic single malt; in its maturation Milk & Honey aim to exemplify the effect of the hot climate of a vibrant Tel-Aviv. Well, that's what they claim but as I've never visited Tel-Aviv I have to take their word for it, bearing in mind that claims for *terroir* are mildly controversial in the world of whisky.

In addition to the Classic, Milk & Honey offer other cask finishes including sherry, former Islay whisky casks for a peated style and Israeli red wine casks (together the Elements series), all culminating in the ever-changing Apex series of small-batch or single-cask bottlings. Both the Classic and the Elements series are available internationally and offer decent value, especially as they are bottled at 46% abv.

For what is a relatively young whisky, the Classic is an impressive achievement with lashings of spice, oak and fruit to hold your attention. Definitely, Milk & Honey is one to watch.

Israel

50

Distillery	Puni
	Puni, Glorenza, Bolzano
Visitor Centre	Yes
Website	www.puni.com

Whisky	
Where	
When	
Verdict	

Puni

I can think of a few contenders for the title of most stunning distillery architecture. Mackmyra would be up there; Abasolo makes the top table; Warenghem is a contender; but top billing has to go to Puni. This is a distillery as *Star Trek*'s Borgs might build it; an uncompromisingly stark and modern construction. While the inspiration may have been the family's love of Scotland and Scotch whisky and the still came from Forsyths,* the architecture has very definitely moved on.

In the hills and glens Puni's 13-metre red-brick cube would cause more of a stir than an ice ball in a glass of single malt. Not to mention maturation in warehouses incorporating World War 2 bunkers, though they also have some above-ground storage.

Construction started in 2010, the still first ran in February 2012 and the initial release of the Nova and Alba expressions were bottled in October 2015. Now, while Italy may seem an unusual place to find a whisky distillery, it's not in fact as outlandish as it may seem. Italians have long had a great love of fine whiskies; Glen Grant built its reputation here (and is now owned by the Campari people); they were early adopters of Macallan, and the Italian bottlers Samaroli have an almost legendary reputation, especially for their 1966 Bowmore Bouquet. A bottle of that – if you could find one – would set you back at least £50,000.

Happily, though not easily found beyond Italy, bottles of Puni are somewhat more affordable though whether they will prove as spectacular an investment I would not care to speculate. Though as you can pick one up in the UK for less than 0.0015 per cent of that amount I daresay more than a few bottles of the early releases have been tucked away by the Gollums of the whisky world.

Shame, really, as the very striking bottle (what else did you expect from Italy?) deserves to be seen, not locked away, and the whisky is both elegant and delicate, as befits a national palate introduced to the delights of the dram by Glen Grant.

---

* While Italian coppersmiths made the stills for the distilleries on the Isles of Harris and Raasay (see 69) it's gratifying to see some business in the opposite direction.

51

Distillery
Visitor Centre
Website

Chichibu
Chichibu, Saitama
No
www.facebook.com/ChichibuDistillery

Whisky

Where

When

Verdict

Chichibu

Here in the decadent West we tend to get rather excited about father-and-son distilling dynasties; respect those that last more than two generations, and revere companies that have remained in family hands for any longer. So meet a man – Ichiro Akuto – who is the 21st generation of his family in the drinks industry. Unfortunately, the family business went bankrupt, but Akuto ended up buying up the old stocks of whisky with the eventual aim of building his own distillery.

Which, in 2007, he did, and in the previous edition of this book I concluded thus: Take note now: although small, this is going to become an increasingly important player in the European scene for Japanese whiskies. Expect to see this name on many, many award citations in the near future.

Well, I was right and really should have stashed away as many bottles as I could. Prices have soared since then, and in a vivid demonstration of the laws of supply and demand this release – the distillery's first 10 Year Old and thus a landmark in their history – falls well into my 'silly' category. That, of course, is a matter of opinion: 'worth' and 'value' are vexed points of contention and entire libraries of books have been written on the 'dismal science'. Back when this whisky was distilled, the distillery was small and that means there are only 5,000 bottles of this to go around. By the time you read this they will be bouncing around auction sites at some enormous profit to those lucky enough to have snared a bottle of the first release.

But such has been Chichibu's success that in 2019 the first spirit ran from a second, greatly enlarged facility, close by the original on which it is modelled, albeit with some small but significant changes: plainly, everything is larger, especially the stills which are now direct fired and the washbacks are constructed from French oak, rather than the Japanese Mizunara of the first distillery.

Greater volumes can be produced here to help meet the apparently insatiable worldwide demand for true Japanese whiskies (see the next entry for details of the new regulations that will help clarify labelling). Let's hope that prices drop somewhat and that this 21st dynasty proves more financially astute than the immediately preceding generations.

Japan

52

Distillery | **Hatozaki**
Visitor Centre | Kaikyo, Akashi City, Hyogo
Website | Under development
| n/a

Whisky	
Where	
When	
Verdict	

Hatozaki

Here's a very fetching bottle with lots of *kanji* script featuring a pagoda-like structure and the words Finest Japanese Whisky. And, remarkably, it could be mine with change from 40 quid. Quite the bargain you may think. But all is not quite as it seems and I'd need the spare cash for soda water.

The Kaikyo Distillery, which maintains a curiously low online profile, is part of the same intensely private Swedish-owned Mossburn Distillers group that owns Torabhaig (see 71). There has been a sake brewery here since 1856 and a distillery on the same site producing Shochu for around a hundred years. It appears though that the original owners, the Yonezawa family, sold all or part of their operations to Mossburn around 2016 and, whatever the precise financial details, they now appear to run the show although Toji (Master Brewer or Distiller) Kimio Yonezawa remains in charge of creating the whiskies.

Mossburn invested substantially in expanding the distilling capacity, bringing in brand-new stills from Forsyths and calling on some heavyweight distilling expertise in the form of Dr Alan Rutherford OBE, a former production director and R&D maestro at DCL and later Diageo. Whisky distilling began here in May 2017 and, at full production, spirit for up to 250,000 bottles of a Family Reserve Single Malt will be produced. It appears, however, that it won't be available until 2022 or 2023.

So what can we buy now?

The Hatozaki Japanese Blended Whisky is widely available, but understand that the Japanese rules controlling 'Japanese whisky' are rather less stringent than those underpinning Scotch or bourbon. In fact, it's perfectly legally permissible to buy bulk whisky from anywhere in the world, ship it to Japan to bottle it and, once exported, it can by some miracle be described as 'Japanese whisky'. All we really know about Hatozaki is that it contains 'both Japanese and foreign distilled malt and grain whiskies', some up to 12 years old, from 'a broad mixture of different cask sizes and types'.

Its light style, cereal notes and slightly sweet palate make it ideal for the popular Highball cocktail which is, of course, why you need the soda water.

STOP PRESS: As this goes to the printers the relevant regulations have been revised and, from March 2024, 'Japanese whisky' will be exactly that. Until then, *caveat emptor*!

Japan

53

Distillery	**Mars** Shinshu Distillery, Miyada, Nr Nagano
Visitor Centre	No
Website	www.hombo.co.jp

Whisky	
Where	
When	
Verdict	

Mars

As I noted in the most recent edition of the companion to this book, *101 Whiskies to Try Before You Die,** though in recent years Japanese whisky has made a remarkable comeback, comparable almost to the revival of Irish whiskey, it gets more and more complex and harder and harder to understand, at least for the '*baka gaijin*' (that's 'stupid foreigner', in which number I am very definitely to be counted). But I expect it's easier for the locals. Hope so, anyway.

Mars' parent company Hombo Shuzo Co. is a small producer of alcoholic beverages. The Mars distillery was opened in 1985 in the modest village of Miyada, around 800 metres above sea level, high up in the Japanese Alps in Nagano, with the aim of producing a whisky with 'special Japanese characteristics'. But read on because this gets confusing. . .

Despite only limited production during the winter, distilling stopped after just seven years and did not resume until 2012 following the general revival in Japanese whiskies. So you have a choice: try to track down some of the original production, which is all but unobtainable and absurdly expensive anyway, or go for something more affordable but more recent.

Now reputedly their Maltage Cosmo made its early impact at the 2015 Tokyo International Bar Show, which comes as a little bit of surprise as like Hatozaki (see 52) this may not be entirely Japanese. Hombo Shuzo have only the one distillery and it would be very unusual for Japanese producers to exchange fillings, as is normal in Scotland, so in all probability some other malts are added. What's more, they don't admit to the percentages or ages of the whiskies involved, leaving the drinker more than a little confused. Though it might feel like sharp practice, right now it's all perfectly legal.

You may feel somewhat short-changed by that, and I'd understand your feelings. The good news is that prices have declined somewhat since this was first available in the West so it represents an accessible gateway of sorts to Japanese whisky. However, following the most recent change to the relevant regulations we may reasonably anticipate that future releases will be more transparent and more authentically Japanese. It's not such a lot to ask.

Japan

54

Distillery Abasolo
Destilería y Bodega Abasolo, Jilotepec
Visitor Centre Yes
Website www.abasolowhisky.com

Whisky

Where

When

Verdict

MIXTAMALIZED
ACCORDING TO
ANCIENT
TRADITIONS

ANCESTRAL
CORN
WHISKY

COPPER
POT
DISTILLED

ALMA DE LA TIERRA

ABASOLO™

EL WHISKY DE MEXICO

100% ANCESTRAL CORN

HECHO EN MEXICO

CRAFTED USING THE FINEST CACAHUAZINTLE CORN,
CULTIVATED OVER GENERATIONS FOR ITS DISTINCTIVE
FLAVOR, RESULTING IN A RICH AND SMOOTH WHISKY.

(86 PROOF)
43% VOL.

DESTILERÍA Y
BODEGA ABASOLO

CONT. NET.
70CL℮

Abasolo

Well, I wasn't expecting this. Whisky seems to have taken over the world. Not satisfied with sending us tequila and mescal, Mexico has now turned its hand to making a corn whisky named Abasolo (though interestingly, the Casa Lumbre company who own it have stuck with the Scottish variant spelling).

The very funky-looking distillery is located in Jilotepec, some 2,400 metres above sea level, and was built from scratch for this project. So you can't deny the scale of the ambition to introduce whisky enthusiasts to a product the distillers describe as 'extremely unique in taste and process, but . . . highlighting the rich heritage and culture of Mexico'.

Since barley isn't a typical Mexican crop the heritage comes from cacahuazintle, an ancient corn variety which grows on high, elevated valleys and is typically used to make pozole, esquites and corn bread. The kernels are then processed in a 4,000 year-old cooking technique known as nixtamalisation. 'There is no whisky in the world with a process or taste profile like this,' say the distillers and I don't suppose the Scotch Whisky Association will be challenging them on that.

Interviewing creator Dr Ivan Saldaña over video, I learned not just of his deeply felt respect for established distilling traditions but his commitment to creating something distinctively Mexican. And I commend that absolutely, as being the whole raison d'être of making a new whisky in a new place with no established whisky tradition.

If you're curious there's no need to hesitate: bottled at 43% abv, the cool-looking 70-cl bottle shouldn't cost more than £40 in the UK and is also widely available in the US. As it's bound to offend single-malt snobs, it's definitely worth it for shock value alone. But is it any good?

Well, strap in because it is something completely different. Abasolo clearly succeeds in the intention to make something unique and representative of a culture and *terroir*. Though some might not care for its raw edges, for me they're part of the point and the charm and the excitement – and I will also be watching to see how this matures with a couple of years' further aging. Don't compare it to US corn whiskies or bourbon. It's a Mexican whisky. That's the whole point.

Mexico

55

Distillery	**Frysk Hynder**
	Us Heit, Bolsward,
	The Netherlands
Visitor Centre	Yes
Website	www.usheitdistillery.nl

Whisky	
Where	
When	
Verdict	

Frysk Hynder

Despite this being the original Dutch whisky, and whisky proving popular in The Netherlands (two whisky magazines and a number of important whisky festivals), it appears that little has been heard of Frysk Hynder elsewhere since my first and last encounter in 2011, and today I'm unable to find it listed anywhere in the UK. Still, as Thomas Gray* reminds us.

> *Full many a flower is born to blush unseen,*
> *And waste its sweetness on the desert air.*

It may well be that we are starved of this Frisian delicacy so that others may drink their fill. However, local production is growing, with ten or more small producers in Holland now, and Millstone (see 56) very much to the fore. Despair ye not, therefore, if Dutch whisky is next on your bucket list.

The Us Heit distillery ('Our Father') was founded by Aart van der Linde following an internship in Scotland (note to Scottish distillers: you might have to stop doing this, that's how the Japanese whisky industry got started) and was first into the local market, releasing a 3-year-old Frysk Hynder expression in 2005.

A variety of wood types including red wine, sherry, port or cognac casks are used and bottles carry detailed information on a side label to gladden the heart of the most obsessive of enthusiasts, detailing the malt type, mashman, date of distillation, stillman, cask type and number, bottling date, strength and so on.

And there, it would seem, matters rest, with the single exception of a cask-strength variant that is matured for an additional two years before bottling. A short video on their website shows some rather unusual stills, and the company also makes a range of Frysk Famke liqueurs and operates a larger brewery.

I recall my admittedly very limited tasting as . . . not memorable at all. I may be blind to its merits and this I freely acknowledge is hardly the most compelling tasting note of all time, but, as an even greater poet† tells us, '*They also serve who only stand and wait.*'

The Netherlands

---

* Thomas Gray 'Elegy Written in a Country Churchyard' (1751).
† John Milton 'When I Consider How my Light is Spent' (1652).

56

Distillery

Visitor Centre
Website

Millstone
Zuidam, Baarle-Nassau,
The Netherlands
No
www.zuidam.eu

Whisky

Where

When

Verdict

Millstone

I know there are rather a lot of rye whiskies in this book, but that's how the world scene rolls. It's a style all on its own, and one you should get to know. It strikes me there are two reasons why the new-wave distillers like it: well made, it's delicious but it's difficult to make well, so there's an element of showing off involved.

The spicy rye is a tricky grain to work with and needs a lot of skill and attention to every stage of the distillation process to get it just right. Get it wrong and you can end up with a porridge-like mess stuck to your mash tun. Zuidam have managed it superbly well.

Small and family-owned, they make quite a range of products including Genever, rum, liqueurs, very, very good gin (let's not forget that gin's story begins in the Netherlands) and, for the last 20 years or so, whiskies including a variety of cask-finished single malts under their Millstone brand that I could happily recommend.

But if we're talking about well-made whiskies, their 100 Rye is a standout. The first time I tried it I simply couldn't believe how tasty it was, and I found it hard to accept that it hadn't been distilled in the USA, rye's traditional home. I then had the considerable pleasure of introducing it to some Dutch people, and they too were impressed and frankly incredulous that it was distilled by their countrymen.

The label doesn't let go of the '100' message, pointing out that this is 100° proof (i.e. 50% abv), and made with 100 per cent rye grain (49% malted, 51% not), in small copper pot stills, aged in 100 per cent new American oak casks and matured for 100 months (that's just over eight years, to save you working it out). In fact, they might as well have given themselves 100/100 on the label and been done with it.

The key flavour is spice: think cinnamon, cloves, vanilla beans – a whole spice market of flavours, overlaid with ripe fruit and hints of cedar wood.

It has rightly won a number of top awards, and as something of a trailblazer I expect it will continue to do so.

57

Distillery | **Cardrona**
Cardrona, Near Wanaka,
South Island
Visitor Centre | Yes
Website | www.cardronadistillery.com

Whisky

Where

When

Verdict

The Cardrona
SINGLE MALT WHISKY

Growing Wings

| MATURED/2020 BOTTLED | #101 Oloroso Sherry Butt CASK | 61.7% ALC/VOL |
| DISTILLED/2015 CASKED | | 0001/1268 BOTTLE |

NEW ZEALAND

UNFILTERED, NATURAL CASK STRENGTH, ALL NATU...

Cardrona

Looking at pictures and the distillery's promotional video, my mind kept going back to Arran and Harris. The distillery architecture, layout and stills seemed uncannily familiar – no surprise really, as the principal components of the whisky operation came from Forsyths of Rothes, supplier of choice to the world's small distillers.

A former farmer, Desiree Whitaker, sold a farm business to travel to the USA and Scotland to study distilling. Building began in January 2015 and the first spirit ran just ten months later. Gin and vodka are also produced but the first whisky wasn't released until three years and a day in cask. However, wasting no time, by 2019 Cardrona was on sale in Australia and the UK. You might encounter the cask-strength Just Hatched in a variety of wood types or, more likely, Growing Wings, a 5 Year Old also released as single casks, at around 60% abv.

However, look out: price alert! These are presented in attractive half bottles (35 cl) in a stylish wooden frame. They look great, but then so they should at the equivalent of over £200 for a standard bottle. This is extremely brave pricing from a new distillery in a country with few distilling credentials at a substantial distance from the world's whisky consumers and entering a crowded, competitive and price-aware market. I can see that there's been a substantial investment here; the packaging is elegant and stylish and the bottles have a long way to come, but this does seem a lot to ask for a young and totally unknown whisky.

In fairness, it's a pretty decent, tasty drop and, given the background, an impressive achievement: there's quite a lot going on in the glass, with an attractive nose, plenty of body and the depth and complexity of drams from more established competitors with high reputations. All great indicators for a positive future for Cardrona and I wish them well.

Perhaps the curiosity factor will carry this off, but long-term success in the drinks business requires consumers to come back for a second and many subsequent bottles, and I can't help but observe that, as I write, I can buy a 25-year-old Glenfarclas single malt for around £125 including delivery. Glenfarclas just celebrated its 185th anniversary. These two facts may be related.

New Zealand

58

Distillery

Visitor Centre
Website

Thomson
Thomson Distillery, Riverhead,
Auckland
No
www.thomsonwhisky.com

Whisky	
Where	
When	
Verdict	

Thomson

Once upon a time (well, 1980 actually, which I appreciate is almost geologically ancient in whisky time) there was a *New Zealand Whisky Book*, which chronicled the rise and poignant fall of a once-buoyant industry established largely by expatriate Scots. The final blow came with the closure of Dunedin's Willowbank distillery in 1997. Curiously, though, no one took much interest in the stock until a husband-and-wife team decided to start their own independent bottler operation and brought a few casks to the market. 'Treasure hunting' they called it.

It proved to be liquid gold – and in 2010 another group moved in to buy up everything remaining. That left our independent bottler friends with a problem so, nothing daunted, Mathew and Rachael Thomson bought a small Portuguese still to start a distillery and New Zealand whisky was reborn.

Rather than ape other styles, the aim was to create something of quality that was distinctively New Zealand. That led to the use of South Island barley kilned over Manuka wood smoke, widely used in New Zealand barbecue cooking as an indigenous alternative to peat smoking, though the maltsters had to devise totally new methods to get the correct balance of flavours in the finished malt.

The early releases of their 'Progress Report' bottlings found immediate acceptance and a raft of awards followed; so too for their South Island peat expression and the Two Tone, so called for the use of former New Zealand red-wine European oak casks and American white oak used exclusively for whisky. As one might expect, all are non-chill filtered, and free of added colour.

Looking to the future, the distillery was expanded in 2018 and the Thomsons are aiming to develop a New Zealand regional style with more extended aging, possibly up to a 10 Year Old. Their Manuka smoke expressions sets a bar for this and, indeed, other New Zealand distillers have followed with their interpretation of this unique whisky which is, quite definitely, smoky.

A modest export effort has followed their award success and Thomson whisky has been shipped to Japan and now the UK, where I am confident it will find an enthusiastic following.

New Zealand

59

Distillery	**Abhainn Dearg**
Visitor Centre	Abhainn Dearg, Carnish, Isle of Lewis
Website	Yes
	www.abhainndeargdistillery.co.uk

Whisky	
Where	
When	
Verdict	

Abhainn Dearg

Let's face it, the island of Lewis (it's in the Outer Hebrides, next stop the USA) is pretty remote. So when you find out that once you've got to Stornoway, it takes over an hour to drive to Abhainn Dearg (Red River in English), you might wonder why anyone would put a distillery there. I certainly did but, take it from me, it would be worth a journey twice as long.

It's the brainchild of local entrepreneur Mark Tayburn. As he tells it, he was concerned that the 2011 Royal National Mod, a festival of Scottish Gaelic song, arts and culture, better known to one and all as the 'Whisky Olympics', would be held in Stornoway without there being any locally distilled whisky to drink. Or any legally distilled whisky anyway. So he determined to remedy this by building a distillery in time for the thirsty delegates' arrival.

It has now passed its tenth anniversary, which is a remarkable and noteworthy achievement and one absolutely to be celebrated. To be honest, despite having visited many, many distilleries in the course of what I laughably refer to as my 'work', I still have the clearest and fondest memory of Abhainn Dearg.

That's because it seems to me, in an age obsessed by health and safety, corporate mission statements and virtue-signalling social media feeds, to carry the soul of whisky close to its heart. It's a time machine to a delightfully simpler age and we should all treasure it. Just to be clear, I loved my visit and look forward to returning just as soon as circumstances permit.

It is, of course, tiny; it has a capacity to produce around 20,000 litres of spirit annually (not to come over all technical, but that's *really* small). What's more, this is a true field-to-bottle operation, with the distillery's own barley – old-school Golden Promise – grown on the island at Nelbost.

Abhainn Dearg Ten is, as you can probably guess, their 10-year-old single malt. You might find it on the shelves of a very dedicated specialist retailer but I'd suggest you go direct and buy off the distillery's website. That's much better for them and more exciting for you (I promise I'll try to get out more).

Scotland

135

60

Distillery
Visitor Centre
Website

Whisky

Where

When

Verdict

Annandale

Once, quite by accident, I bought a derelict distillery. In its day it had been important but nothing remained save a tumbledown building so I retired to a dark and quiet place, put a towel over my head and relinquished any idea of resuming operations. Others are not so timid.

But it is as well that I did as, in discovering Annandale, I have realised that I would have to address such vexing issues as the conceptual consonance of my brand personality. If you're interested in such matters there is a very clear exposition of both the theory and practice that underlies Annandale's branding on their website, where we learn that the names and packaging of their two mainline single malts are the creation of some quite advanced mathematical modelling combined with the designers' intuition.

Annandale first opened in 1836, closed – apparently permanently – in 1924 and was revived by the current owners, the husband-and-wife team of Professor David Thomson and Teresa Church in 2014. Mind you, it took them seven years and many millions of pounds to produce anything. As a one-time owner of an abandoned distillery, I salute their courage, strength and indefatigability, not to mention their grasp of statistical modelling.

You'll have gathered there's a lot of serious science behind everything they do. The distillery is no exception and, like many others, they utilised the services of Dr Jim Swan in their early planning. His influence, especially regarding STR casks, is still felt, though Annandale now stands very firmly on its own two feet.

Suffice it to say that the whisky, guided initially by some shrewd descriptive sensory analysis, is excellent. The Man o'Words references Robert Burns and the peated Man o'Sword is a tribute to Robert the Bruce, Scottish heroes both with links to Annandale's Lowland home. There are also, at a price, very limited quantities remaining of the initial vintages.

In March 2021 it was announced that the distillery had pre-sold half their annual production to a finance company who will sell individual casks to the public on an investment basis. Quite what this will mean for future availability and prices remains to be seen but, in my opinion at least, it's a worrying development.

Scotland

61

Distillery	**Arbikie**
	Arbikie Highland Estate Distillery,
	Inverkeilor, Arbroath
Visitor Centre	Yes
Website	www.arbikie.com

Whisky	
Where	
When	
Verdict	

HIGHLAND RYE

RELEASE: 2020

ARBIKIE HIGHLAND RYE 1794

SINGLE GRAIN SCOTCH WHISKY

700ml | 48% vol

Arbikie

A field-to-bottle farm distillery producing the only Scottish rye whisky available in the world. That's got to be interesting.

Arbikie is in Angus, great farming country but largely by-passed by the tourist hordes (who thereby miss a rather lovely if under-rated part of Scotland). Though a distillery dating from 1794 can be found on old maps and the Stirling family have been farming here since the 1920s, distilling only started in 2015 when new Master Distiller Kirsty Black began making vodka and gin.

The entrepreneurial Stirling family, owners of this 2,500-acre estate, brought in German Carl stills alongside Ms Black's distilling skills, and whisky production began in late 2015, though the first release of single malt is not anticipated to be until 2029.

In the meantime, we can enjoy releases of their Arbikie Highland Rye 1794 with no age declaration or Arbikie Highland Rye Single Grain Scotch Whisky at four years of age, which is distilled from a combination of estate-grown Arantes Scottish rye with wheat and malted barley, before being matured in a combination of charred American oak casks and ex-Armagnac barrels.

Two things stand out here: firstly, Arbikie's research into historic distilling records show that rye grain was used in Scotch whisky production until the late nineteenth century. That's an interesting link to an under-discussed and little-known part of whisky's history, providing Arbikie with cultural heritage and a degree of provenance. But secondly, and probably more important in today's market, is the commendable transparency of the packaging. The label offers the wealth of detail on the whisky's background that enthusiast consumers rightly demand, and as the grain can be tracked to the exact Arbikie field where it grew there are gratifyingly few food miles involved in its production.

However, it must be acknowledged that the price – £250 online at the time of writing for the 4 Year Old and £130 for the unaged 1794 expression – is a problem, especially when compared to prices of around £40 for the gin and vodka. Is it possible that white spirits are the priority with whisky more of a curiosity? Only time will tell, though full marks for fresh thinking.

Scotland

62

Distillery Daftmill
Visitor Centre No
Website www.daftmill.com

Daftmill
Daftmill, By Cupar, Fife

Whisky	
Where	
When	
Verdict	

Daftmill

As we shall shortly discover at Lindores (see 67), distilling started with holy men. But, before long, farmers took it over and until the middle of the nineteenth century, small farm distilleries were commonplace across Scotland.

Sadly, that's no longer the case – but there are notable exceptions. And my prize exhibit is Daftmill, which is coincidentally quite close to Lindores and thus categorised as a Lowland single malt.

So you've got to admire how Daftmill did their thing. No crowdfunding. No selling casks of new make at highly inflated prices. Nothing from the public purse and nothing rushed onto the market. No slick PR messages about their 'journey' and no sign of the dreaded p-word. There's not even one of those entirely fatuous age filters on the website.

The Cuthbert family has farmed here for six generations. Today, besides distilling whisky, they grow potatoes and their own malting barley and have a fine herd of beef cattle. The distillery is housed in a handsome old mill building where the barley is distilled.

I interviewed Francis Cuthbert about the project shortly after they had built their distillery. Back then he distilled everything himself, very slowly, working to a traditional farm pattern of three months on, with three months off, to fit around other farming activity such as planting and harvesting. Today, around a hundred casks of spirit are distilled annually, though Daftmill is capable of several times that if farming schedules permit.

Right from the beginning they made the decision to wait a full ten years for their whisky to mature. That's financially very brave.

In fact, it took 12 years before the first release left the distillery and there were only 629 bottles – 'rarer than rocking horse shit' they say. Quantities are still incredibly limited but, taking that into account and despite the high bottling strength, prices are very reasonable.

Releases are generally one-offs with specialists such as London's Berry Bros & Rudd, Master of Malt, local Fife retailers Abbey Whisky and France's top whisky experts La Maison du Whisky. As far as I can see they don't appear on auction sites with any frequency, suggesting that people are drinking them. Hallelujah! Watch very closely, move very fast and you might get very lucky.

Scotland

63

Distillery	**Eden Mill**
	Eden Mill, Guardbridge,
	St Andrews, Fife
Visitor Centre	Yes
Website	www.edenmill.com

Whisky	
Where	
When	
Verdict	

Eden Mill

Eden Mill are enlightened enough to be a sponsor of Hibernian FC. Admittedly, Hibs are renowned for their ability to consistently stumble just as meaningful achievement is within their grasp (the magnificent 3-2 victory over a well-known Glasgow club in the 2016 Scottish Cup Final being a noteworthy exception), and the sponsorship is for Eden Mill's gin - but the long-suffering supporters of Leith's finest must take what comfort they can get, even if it's Mother's Ruin.

Encouragingly though, this little distillery is now making single-malt whisky and has ambitious £7-million plans for expansion with the aim of becoming Scotland's first carbon-neutral distillery. Located within the University of St Andrews' Guardbridge campus, power and heat for the stills will be supplied by biomass, with solar panels on the distillery roof. Already it's one of the very few that combine a brewery with distilling; a ruthlessly logical and commercially compelling combination that is remarkably unusual given both the historic links and obvious production synergies that we also see at Canadian Victoria Caledonian (see 18).

In actual fact, the brewery came first and distilling followed in 2014 with the first single malt, which very quickly sold out, launched in 2018. Head Distiller Scott Ferguson is nothing if not experimental in his approach, using bourbon, Pedro Ximénez and oloroso barrels as well as spirit distilled with Pale, Chocolate, Brown and Crystal Malt Barley in the most recent expression. However, what's the point in running a boutique operation if you don't have the freedom and confidence to explore the rich and varied possibilities of cask and grain?

In that spirit, the website offers small (20 cl) sample bottles in what they term the Hip Flask series. At £30 they're a really great way to get to know the distillery; discover your personal preferences for cask type, finish and so on. It's an excellent initiative that I wish more distilleries would copy, not least because these small bottles will likely be drunk by committed enthusiasts and not locked up in some ghastly investment collection (apologies for going on but this investment thing makes my teeth itch). Sadly, though, I don't suppose the very first Eden Mill single malt, sold at auction for £7,100, will ever see a glass in action.

Scotland

143

64

Distillery

Visitor Centre
Website

Glasgow
The Glasgow Distillery Company,
Hillington, Glasgow
No
www.glasgowdistillery.com

Whisky	
Where	
When	
Verdict	

Glasgow

Just like buses in the rain, you wait for years for a Glasgow distillery and then three come along almost at once. With both the Clutha and Clydeside distilleries located more centrally, they have an obvious interest in the potential for tourism income but the Glasgow Distillery Company stands apart from them. Firstly, by opening first it was able to secure the naming rights that link it to the city's long whisky heritage, and secondly, it's not open to the public.

I'd hazard a guess that this relates to its location in Hillington Business Park, in a building with a gritty look far removed from the picture-postcard image that single malt likes to portray. Funding for the business has come from a group of Asian food and drink investors as well as a Regional Selective Assistance grant. Apparently, an investment of 'several million' pounds was involved in total. However, it's the liquid we care about, so let's see.

First out of the blocks was Makar gin (Scots for 'poet'), then some third-party bottlings, followed by Glasgow 1770 Single Malt. This lays claim to being the first Glasgow-distilled single malt since the closure of Dundashill around a century ago – the link being that it was established in 1770 and the Glasgow Distillery Company aims to re-establish a metropolitan malt-distilling tradition mirroring the classic production regions, thus bringing Glasgow malt whisky back to life.

The Glasgow 1770 was launched in June 2018 and now exists in three variants: The Original, Peated and Triple Distilled, released in May 2020. These latter expressions hark back to the original Lowland style of triple distillation, which today we normally associate with Irish whiskey. It's not unknown in Scotland though and Auchentoshan, Rosebank, and the Campbeltown Hazelburn from Springbank all offer a triple-distilled style.

Like its counterparts in the city, the Glasgow Distillery is backed by serious, experienced and well-connected drinks industry executives and is evidently well funded. If you doubt that, just take a look at the stylish customised bottle. Designs and a new bespoke glass mould don't come cheap so this is a big statement of intent. My sole cavil is that they've adopted the smaller 50-cl bottle but it's a welcome return for the 'Weegies'.

Scotland

65

Distillery Glen Scotia
Visitor Centre Glen Scotia, Campbeltown, Argyll
Website Yes
www.glenscotia.com

Whisky	
Where	
When	
Verdict	

Glen Scotia

Call me sentimental if you must, but as my text approached completion I realised there was nothing from Scotland with a 'Glen' in its name and, more significantly, nothing from Campbeltown. This, of course, is for the very good reason that distilleries called Glen tend to be large and well known and furthermore because no one is currently distilling on a boutique scale in Campbeltown (someone should).

But Glen Scotia is not large, indeed there are larger world distilleries included here, and as Campbeltown once laid claim to being the whisky capital of the world I claim your indulgence.

Glen Scotia stands as a proud survivor from the days when around 30 distilleries were working here. In 1930, when Campbeltown's sad decline had already begun, Aeneas MacDonald described these 'potent, full-bodied, pungent whiskies' as 'the double basses of the whisky orchestra'. There is a somewhat better-known neighbour at Springbank but Glen Scotia's revival under the recent new ownership of the Loch Lomond Group merits its inclusion.

Since they acquired the distillery in 2014 there has been steady and thoughtful investment in the restoration of the antiquated equipment, some upgrading, an increase in capacity and warehouse space and the creation of a small visitor centre. The packaging has been sensitively redesigned and we've seen a steady stream of releases ranging from the UK supermarket exclusive Glen Scotia Harbour (which, if you're lucky, can be found at £25) up to the 45-year-old single malt. At close to £4,000 it's a lot of money, but quite the bargain considering its rarity and when compared to other aged malts, few of which have this storied history.

For the most part, the whiskies are sensibly priced. The cask-strength Victoriana appeals to the romantic in me: it doesn't carry an age statement but is drawn from a very limited cask selection and is packed full of fruits, spice and well-balanced woody notes from the deep charred barrels. If you can't get to Campbeltown, which you should do once, there's an excellent and very clear video on the website. Manager Iain McAlister shows why here at least the stillman remains a skilled and valued operator, not a slave to a computer programme.

Scotland

66

Distillery

Visitor Centre
Website

Kingsbarns
Kingsbarns Distillery, Kingsbarns,
Nr St Andrews, Fife
Yes
www.kingsbarnsdistillery.com

Whisky	
Where	
When	
Verdict	

Kingsbarns

The first time I saw Kingsbarns, a number of years ago, it was tipping down. Rainwater was coming through the roof and most of the building – then the half-derelict shell of a disused 'petting farm' for children – looked ready to collapse. Unfortunately for the promoters who saw a distillery there, the eighteenth-century buildings were protected for their historic value and architectural interest and couldn't be demolished making way for a new structure, so I didn't give it much of a chance.

But, since my first visit, there are completely new owners; all the previous team have departed and the distillery has been completely redesigned. Kingsbarns vividly illustrates the challenges, frustrations and satisfactions of trying to get a new project off the ground. Would-be distillers can learn from this story.

Now financed primarily by the Wemyss family, local aristos and proprietors of the independent bottlers of the same name, the simple and elegant distillery is relatively small, but can produce around 200,000 original litres of spirit annually, with all the grain grown locally in Fife, some on the family's own land.

Once again, we may detect the hand of the late Dr Jim Swan, who along with Ian Palmer (another very experienced Master Distiller of note) advised on the distillery design, yeast strains and, vitally, the use of STR Portuguese wine barriques and other high-quality casks.

The first whisky was distilled as recently as March 2015, the aim being to produce a light and fruity spirit in what is described as the 'traditional Lowland style'. With the Dream to Dram, they've succeeded: this is indeed a light and fruity whisky, but one with charm that I believe will age well.

On the nose, there are notes of apricot, peach and grapefruit with hints of a toasted brioche; the palate is medium bodied, with suggestions of a custard tart with stewed plums, toffee and red fruits. At 46% abv it will hold some water but is easy to sip neat – naturally, it is non-chill filtered and bottled at its natural pale colour. The sister brand Balcomie is a 5-year-old 100 per cent oloroso-sherry-butt-matured expression full of nuts and fruit – move on to this once you've tried Dream to Dram.

67

Distillery	**Lindores Abbey**
	Lindores Abbey Distillery,
	Newburgh, Fife
Visitor Centre	Yes
Website	www.lindoresabbeydistillery.com

Whisky	
Where	
When	
Verdict	

Lindores Abbey

OK, so this isn't whisky as such. It's a 'spirit drink', a sort of bucket category in alcohol regulations to describe something that isn't one of the recognised, mainstream categories.

But if it was good enough for King James IV of Scotland and the Tironensian monk Friar John Cor of Lindores Abbey, then it deserves your attention. Mind you, that was in 1494. A passing mention in medieval court Latin in the Exchequer Rolls of Scotland (sort of an account book for the royal household) means Lindores is widely acknowledged as the home of Scotch whisky. The good Friar is recorded as having been sent eight bolls of malt to make aqua vitae. That's enough, it's thought, for a present-day distiller to make around 1,500 bottles so we can reasonably presume some sort of craft-distilling operation here over five centuries ago.

Mind you, a Reformation mob led by John Knox destroyed everything in 1559 and there's a reasonable argument that the *modern* whisky industry owes more to the very large, late-eighteenth-century distilleries at Kennetpans and Kilbagie, now sadly derelict. Certainly no one took very much notice of Lindores until the present owners of the site, the McKenzie Smith family, built their rather smart distillery and visitor centre and began distilling in December 2017. Commendably, they've taken the decision not to release any whisky until it's at least five years old so there won't be any available until late 2021, though if you simply can't wait, they have released limited quantities of the new make.

Aqua Vitae seeks to provide some sense of what the King and his court would have been drinking. Lucky them, because this is tasty stuff and great in cocktails, or simply served long and cold with a decent ginger ale. What's more, while many in the craft-distilling world quickly launched some gin, here the 'journey' (sigh) is on the road less travelled by, but with a clear link to its origin and long history.

While you're probably tired of hearing this, Dr Jim Swan advised on building the distillery and operating the stills. And he had forgotten more about distilling than some old monk ever knew.

Scotland

151

68

Distillery	**Nc'Nean**
	Nc'nean, Nc'nean Distillery, Drimnin
Visitor Centre	Yes
Website	www.ncnean.com

Whisky	
Where	
When	
Verdict	

Nc'Nean

If you're going to build the one-hundredth-and-something distillery in Scotland you need something to make you stand out. For me, it's the relentlessly woke virtue signalling all over Nc'nean's website but then I am pretty high in the gammon stakes. I know about brand positioning, segmentation and targeting (believe me, I've walked that walk and got the redundancy notice) but here the strategy hangs out a mile wide. Fair enough, because this whisky is evidently intended for someone other than me.

These folks are, and I quote, 'uninhibited', 'pioneering' and 'experimental'. They 'walk their own path' and are 'made by nature not by rules' (don't anyone tell the Scotch Whisky Association).

Heady stuff. But read on, because it gets better.

Their aim apparently is 'to change the way the world thinks about whisky from Scotland'. They are 'protectors of nature' and – woo woo alert – have a guiding star, one Neachneohain, a huntress and Queen of Spirits in Gaelic legend. Or, as Sir Walter Scott would have it, 'a gigantic and malignant female'.

I thought by now that I'd drifted onto goop.com, for this is surely whisky as Gwyneth Paltrow would reimagine it. Tell it not in the glens of Morvern, but they hae a guid conceit o' thirsels at Nc'nean where they're aye vauntie.

But I was impressed by their efforts to minimise their environmental footprint – biomass boiler, organic barley, recycled glass bottle (five stars for that) and the wholly admirable fact that you can save £2 on a bottle by choosing not to have the outer tube – until I realised that they bottle on site. So all those dry goods (bottle, cork, tube, carton, pallet etc.) have to be trucked in over some quite challenging roads, bottled and then all trucked out again in large lorries – fuelled presumably by good intentions.

It may be of interest that while the CEO's family own the estate on which the distillery has been built, substantial sums of taxpayers' money have gone into the project, along with crowdfunding and advance cask sales with prices starting at £3,500 (that's before bottling costs, duty, VAT and transportation).

Oh, and Jim Swan helped out here as well.

Scotland

153

69

Distillery	**Raasay**
	Isle of Raasay, Borodale House, Raasay
Visitor Centre	Yes
Website	www.raasaydistillery.com

Whisky	
Where	
When	
Verdict	

Raasay

Raasay is an agreeable small Hebridean island, easily accessed by a small ferry from Skye. As you approach the jetty, look up and to your right and that's your destination: a ten-minute walk to an old hotel that's been extended and converted to smart private accommodation for visitors to the distillery, an uncompromisingly modern new-build immediately next to the reception area.

Though local Gaelic place names reflect a heritage of moonshining, this represents the first legal distilling here in history. The distillery is the brainchild of Alasdair Day and his business partner Bill Dobbie who are also behind the Tweeddale blended whisky and hope eventually to open a second distillery in the Scottish borders.

Raasay opened in September 2017 and so its whisky is coming of age now. The inaugural release was well received and, developing the theme of provenance, the aim is for future expressions to be produced using Raasay-grown and malted barley, dried using local peat to create a 100 per cent Isle of Raasay Single Malt. Notably, this will be the first barley grown on the island in a generation and represents a significant step to a true field-to-bottle operation.

The distillery itself, though compact, can produce just under 200,000 litres annually, the current practice being to mature all output in the adjacent warehouses, where they have a considerable variety of different casks available for finishing. There is a private cask scheme with a very clear and transparent offer of different cask types that may be accessed from the website. They also make gin (of course).

Such has been the demand for equipment that (like the somewhat larger Isle of Harris distillery, opened a couple of years earlier) the stills have come from the Italian firm Stilli who must be thoroughly delighted with the explosion of new distilleries in Scotland.

With tourism of vital importance to many new ventures, Raasay are collaborating with Harris and Torabhaig (see 71) and Talisker on Skye to promote a Hebridean Whisky Trail which, pre-pandemic, had got off to an impressive start.

While Raasay is a little out of the way, I thought it quite charming in scale and style and well worth the detour; all in all, a great addition to Scotland's distilling landscape.

Scotland

155

70

Distillery

Visitor Centre
Website

Strathearn
Strathearn Distillery, Bachilton Farm
Steading, Methven, Perth
Under development
www.strathearndistillery.com

Whisky

Where

When

Verdict

Strathearn

Strathearn was opened in August 2013 and claimed at that time to be 'probably Scotland's smallest distillery'. Frankly, I'm not sure who cares and anyway, as soon as you say this, someone comes along who's even more diminutive – big deal. It now makes an even bigger claim for itself; suggesting that this is 'Scotland's original craft spirits distillery'. But let's leave that there and acknowledge that despite its size Strathearn punches well above its weight and has had a powerful and positive influence on the Scottish craft distilling scene.

That's largely because founder Tony Reeman-Clark played a formative role in establishing the Scottish Craft Distillers Association to encourage growth within the sector and defend the authenticity of Scottish craft spirits (incidentally, something similar is badly needed for England and Wales). With their distinctively styled Portuguese stills from Hoga making both rum and gin as well as Scotch whisky, they have also mentored many aspiring distillers who have gone on to establish their own small distilleries.

So well have they done that they came to the attention of longstanding independent bottlers Douglas Laing, who in their first move into distilling bought Strathearn in October 2019. Strathearn's boutique scale will complement Laing's other operation, the larger Clutha Distillery with company headquarters now under construction in an impressively imposing building on Glasgow's Pacific Quay.

Though Strathearn had made available various malt spirits and new make matured in different woods, there had only been two very limited and expensive releases of single malt prior to the sale of the business. Indeed bottle #001 of the first release sold for a remarkable £4,150 (but Eden Mill got more and the first Nc'nean fetched £41,004 so that's one for the lassies).

Under the new owners, who have more than 70 years' experience of the whisky business and a substantial export trade, the first full release of the single malt came in 2020 shortly after they acquired the business. Packaged with a rather sophisticated label with attractive typography, it's based on whisky distilled in 2013 and 2014 and aged in a combination of European oak and ex-sherry casks. It has been bottled at 46.6% abv and is both of natural colour and non-chill filtered – as it really should be.

Scotland

71

Distillery   Torabhaig
Visitor Centre   Teangue, Sleat, Skye
Website   Yes
   www.torabhaig.com

Whisky	
Where	
When	
Verdict	

Torabhaig

I vividly recall standing in the teeming rain outside a ruined Torabhaig having a heated row with Sir Iain Noble, the then owner, about his plans for the visitor centre. He wanted an open fire with a small still making usquabae which he planned to sell as 'Gaelic whisky' (or some such nonsense) and wouldn't accept my increasingly firmly expressed view that this would not be acceptable to HM Customs and Excise, let alone the fire-safety officer. We were both adamant in our strongly held opinions and stuck to them as we got progressively wetter and wetter. Later he refused to pay me but, before I could sue him, he died. After that there seemed little prospect of the farmhouse distillery he envisaged for this delightful 1820s farmhouse steading ever being built.

But wait! His estate sold the project on to Mossburn Distillers, a subsidiary of Marussia Beverages BV, itself a holding company for the privately owned Swedish group Haydn Holding AB who also own the Reivers Distillery in the Scottish Borders, Kaikyo in Japan (see 52) and other spirit brands.

Behind this complex web we find the Paulsen Family Foundation, a legal entity incorporated in Jersey and one seriously rich individual, Sir Frederick Paulsen Jr, a 70-something Swede, biotech pharmaceutical billionaire and, from January 2020, a Knight of the Order of St John in the Priory of England and the Islands, to add to his earlier OBE.

And his team got it done. So now Skye has two whisky distilleries though, with a potential output of 500,000 litres of single malt, Torabhaig is producing on a scale substantially larger than proposed by Sir Iain. It is, in fact, a considerable tribute to the architectural and engineering team involved that they have shoehorned the necessary plant into the historic farmhouse buildings to produce this amount. The set-up is indeed impressive.

The first whisky, from the Legacy Series, has recently been released but the aim is to build stocks so that 10 Year Old and older expressions may eventually be available, based around their flavour template of 'well-tempered peat'.

Strange that this little farmhouse distillery engaged the attention of two Knights of the Realm. No open fire in the visitor centre though.

Scotland

72

Distillery | **Wolfburn**
Visitor Centre | Wolfburn, Thurso, Caithness
Website | Yes
 | www.wolfburn.com

Whisky

Where

When

Verdict

Wolfburn

Wolfburn, which began distilling in January 2013, make great play of their location, stressing that they are 'Scotland's first and last mainland whisky distillery'. Well, so they are – at least until the stills at John o'Groats start running or Dunnet Bay adds whisky to its excellent gin. And Scapa and Highland Park are only a short ferry ride away, not to mention the 'most northerly Scotch whisky distillery', Shetland Reel.

We read a lot of these kind of grand-sounding but essentially meaningless descriptions. Insofar as we can detect *terroir* in whisky, it's derived from the barley; essentially the variety used and where it's grown. The physical location of the stills makes vanishingly little difference. I understand the marketing teams' search for some unique selling proposition but I do wish they'd look further and try harder. The increasingly sophisticated whisky consumer is looking for greater depth and more transparency.

However, well done to Wolfburn. In their relatively short life they've established the brand and launched a decent range of whiskies that are, for the scale of the operation, reasonably priced. What's more, everything is bottled at 46% abv or above and, as stocks mature, we may anticipate whiskies carrying an age statement as opposed to today's NAS (No Age Statement) style. And there's another interesting thing: Wolfburn has been able to attract a distilling team with impressive CVs. The first manager, Shane Fraser, came from Glenfarclas and today's head distiller Iain Kerr is ex-Glenlivet. These are amongst the top companies in the industry so Wolfburn's potential customers may be reassured that production is in skilled hands.

Perhaps it's the appeal of working in a very hands-on way. At 135,000 litres per annum, the distillery's capacity is modest; in fact, it's only slightly larger than the 28,056 'Total Gallons of Proof Spirit' that were produced in 1826 at the original Wolfburn distillery, the ruins of which lie just 350 metres from the present-day site.

While there are a number of small-batch releases under the Kylver label, Northland and Morven are the core expressions – the latter delivers the peat buzz beloved of smokeheads, while the more civilised amongst us tend to the lighter, slightly sweet impact of the ex-bourbon casks used to mature Northland.

Scotland

73

Distillery

Visitor Centre
Website

Three Ships
James Sedgwick, Wellington,
Western Cape
Yes
www.threeshipswhisky.co.za

Whisky	
Where	
When	
Verdict	

Three Ships

With a strong indigenous wine-making industry and many years of economic isolation, it should be no surprise to learn that South Africa has a substantial and well-established distilling industry. Add to that the fact that since the country rejoined the world community, Scotch whisky sales have been booming there once again (historically, this was an important market for blends such as Dewar's and Johnnie Walker, and today South Africa is one of Scotch's largest markets) and one could predict the rise of local whisky distilling. Don't forget, with a substantial wine industry, they've been making excellent brandy for years, though relatively little leaves the country.

Owner Distell Group's James Sedgwick distillery, where they began making whisky in 1990, can be traced back to 1886, and they also have distilling interests in Scotland. Considerable expansion is in hand in Wellington, based on their Three Ships brand, as their whisky continues locally popular and with international interest growing.

In the previous edition I recommended Bain's Cape Mountain grain whisky which is also produced here, and I'm still a fan because we don't see enough grain whiskies. But Master Distiller Andy Watts, a former English county cricketer, has excelled himself with Three Ships Aged 12 Years. The bottle and carton both carry the prominent wording 'Master Distiller's Private Collection'. If so, he's been very generous in sharing this first release. Now coming in at a healthy 46.3% abv, Three Ships (South Africa's first single malt) was originally released as a 10 Year Old but the additional two years' maturation has done it no harm at all. In fact, the warmer climate has accelerated the flavour's development, adding richness and depth to an already very impressive whisky.

At under £50 at the time of writing, you really shouldn't overlook this nicely balanced drop from the only commercial whisky distillery in Africa, highly praised for its sustainability practices and environmental sensitivity. If this had been made in Scotland or any more widely recognised whisky country I'd expect to have to pay considerably more, and I will be fascinated to see how this continues to age. Distell are a large and powerful company, with significant distilling interests in Scotland: Mr Watts has played a fine innings here and Three Ships more than deserves its place in World Whiskies 1st XI.

74

Distillery
Visitor Centre
Website

Embrujo de Granada
Liber, Padul, Granada
Yes
www.destileriasliber.com

Whisky	
Where	
When	
Verdict	

Embrujo de Granada

Though Spain has recently enjoyed a major gin boom, it has long been established as a significant whisky market, largely for standard blends. One would have imagined that there would have been more whisky-orientated activity from their many smaller distillers but though Liber is not the only whisky distillery in Spain (Beam Suntory's DyC is both substantially larger and longer established) it was the first to produce single malt.

Like most distilleries, it makes much of its water source (a particularly hoary old myth; water's origin is largely irrelevant to the final taste) and the considerably more important casks it uses for aging. The end product is known as Embrujo de Granada ('Bewitched by Granada').

Located near the Sierra Nevada mountains, the distillery was established by a small group of enthusiasts supported by friends and family as investors. The stills were created by local craftsmen but closely resemble Scottish pot stills, with a large boiling ball, though with very tall straight necks and shallow lyne arms.

Great stress is placed on cask selection and extended maturation. As might be expected the casks show a strong national influence, being American oak barrels previously used for a Pedro Ximénez sherry solera. With the distillery situated between the slopes of the Sierra Nevada and the Costa Tropical, the local microclimate features alternating temperatures of sub-zero winters and those scorchio! summers which, say the distillery, 'gives our own character and personality [to the] whisky'.

Production started in 2002 and today the Embrujo is bottled as a 10 Year Old. There are also very limited releases of older whiskies bottled at 60% abv for the Spanish Whisky Club. Sadly, it is some while since I have seen any bottles in the UK but that is no reason not to at least try to track one down.

As with many smaller distillers, a range of other liqueurs, rum and vodka is also produced. As an example of the worldwide interest and enthusiasm for single-malt whisky, and proof that it can – with care – be produced virtually anywhere, Embrujo de Granada is of more than passing interest to the enthusiast and a welcome entrant on the world whisky scene. I was certainly bewitched by it.

Spain

75

Distillery	**Gotland**
	Gotland, Romakloster,
	Gotland Island
Visitor Centre	No – visits by appointment
Website	www.gotlandwhisky.se

Whisky	
Where	
When	
Verdict	

Gotland

Why make whisky on an island? It's daft. Well, except on Islay, obviously. Or Skye. Or Tasmania.

So an island in the Baltic, somewhere between Sweden and Latvia, isn't such a surprising idea, especially when you take the Nordic love for whisky into account and remember that there are more than a dozen Swedish whisky distilleries.

Gotland's production dates from 2012, assisted by Harry Cockburn – former production director at Bowmore and also instrumental in helping the Cotswolds Distillery (see 23) get started. But the most striking thing is that the business is owned by more than 2,200 small shareholders who provided the initial funding and working capital. Thanks to them, Gotland operates without borrowing money. As they proclaim with justifiable pride, they own everything, including their pair of Forsyths stills.

As a result, though, the far-sighted and prudent owners get first dibs on the special Shareholders' Edition bottlings and by the time the Swedish government's alcohol-retailing monopoly Systembolaget places its order there's little left for the rest of the world. We can live in hope, though; find a penfriend in Sweden or note that over 8,000 bottles of recent editions such as Isle of Lime Ullahau have been produced.

The brand has its own dedicated website, imaginatively enough at www.isleoflime.com, where every conceivable aspect of each release is listed in painstaking detail. Want to know who was responsible for the technical drawing for the bottle design, or where the corks come from? It's all here, along with a meticulous description of the grain (variety, farm and malting procedure), yeast type and precise descriptions of each and every cask.

So by now, and knowing me knowing you, you probably have a dream of money, money, money and would like to take a chance on becoming an owner. Sadly, the initial share offer was fully subscribed but there is an aftermarket. When I checked on the website, parcels of between 250 and 800 shares were available, generally around 50 Swedish krona per share (not much more than £4). So for rather less than a bottle of Macallan 25 Year Old (which you probably won't even drink) you could be part owner of an island distillery. What's stopping you? After all, the winner takes it all.

76

Distillery | **Mackmyra**
Visitor Centre | Mackmyra Whisky Village, Gävle
Website | Yes
| www.mackmyra.se

Whisky

Where

When

Verdict

MACKMYRA

SVENSK EK

SWEDISH SINGLE MALT WHISKY

Våra ekfat är tillverkade av träd som för hundratals
år sedan planterades på Visingsö för att bli virke till
Sveriges flotta. Idag ger de smak till vårt moderna
och innovativa whiskyhantverk.

ALKOHOLHALT: | VOLYM: | MASTER
46.1% VOL | 70 CL | BLENDER:

Mackmyra

The Swedes have long been whisky enthusiasts but with its creation in 1999 Mackmyra really started something, and today in this country of some 10 million people there are around a dozen distilleries making single malt. After some financial strains Mackmyra has a leading position and now operates from two sites.

The original distillery is now the Lab Distillery, home to their funkier and more experimental spirits, while two core styles of whisky (crudely, one is fruity, the other smoky) are produced in the striking tower of their gravity-fed distillery in the Whisky Village. This is also home to their visitor operation, which offers a range of distillery tours and also a restaurant – sadly, off-licence sales are a Swedish government monopoly, so no souvenir bottles to mark your visit.

Led by Master Blender Angela d'Orazio, they continue to build on a reputation as one of the most innovative and exciting of the new wave of producers, and being of an experimental turn of mind they have an extensive range of whiskies. Despite Mackmyra's enthusiastic and loyal local following, quite a wide range can be found in leading specialists – I counted around a dozen on one site, including some from the Season and Moments range. Supplies can be very limited, however, so if you see one and it appeals it's best to move quickly.

However, probably the lead product and thus the easiest place to start is the Svensk EK, which, quite rightly, has picked up an enviable hat-load of awards. The wood regime underlying this elegant whisky is complex, but includes Swedish oak first grown for shipbuilding and former bourbon barrels. Quarter casks are used to accelerate maturation and a proportion of the casks have been heavily toasted for greater wood character. Mackmyra's restless experimentation continues so the wood policy will doubtless evolve in interesting ways.

When first launched, Mackmyra's whiskies tended to be expensive but as production has expanded (and other whisky prices risen) they look increasingly good value, especially when the undoubted quality and the fact that most are bottled at 46% abv are considered.

77

Distillery

Visitor Centre
Website

Smögen
Smögen, Ståleröd,
Near Hunnebostrand
Yes
www.smogenwhisky.se

Whisky	
Where	
When	
Verdict	

SMÖGEN

SWEDISH SINGLE MALT WHISKY

~ 100 Proof ~

Sherry Quarter Casks

At least **6** years old

Natural colour ~ Non chill filtered ~ 57,1%alc/vol

Smögen

Founded in 2009 by lawyer (boo!) and whisky writer (hurrah!) Pär Caldenby, this small but highly influential Swedish distillery is noted for its commitment to high quality spirit long before any wood influence comes into play and aims unashamedly for BIG flavours.

Which serves as a very good illustration as to why there are no scores or tasting notes to be found in this book. You may recall a scene in the 1984 mockumentary *This is Spinal Tap*, following the purported comeback tour of a fictional British heavy metal band in which guitarist Nigel Tufnel shows the bemused filmmaker the controls on his amplifier, proudly explaining that 'these go to 11'.

And that's what we have here: a combination of heavily peated malt, matured for six years in small oloroso sherry quarter casks and bottled at a fearsome 57.1% abv. If you like Bruichladdich's more outrageous peated whiskies you're going to love this. Fair enough, but I really don't, which would mean a low score and some grudging tasting notes full of references to hot chillies, peppers, barbecued meats and smoke. All good things in moderation, of course, but Smögen don't really aim to do moderation.

However, regardless of my opinion, lots of people love this style and Smögen do it very well indeed, which explains why it's here despite my personal aversion to whisky turned up to 11.

Caldenby himself is in charge of day-to-day production and relentless in his pursuit of the intense flavours he aims to produce. As just one example of his detailed approach, the distillery was designed with cooling equipment on the stills that sought to mimic the effect of traditional worm tubs. These, unfortunately, are considerably more expensive and take up more room than the conventional shell-and-tube type of condensers that are in general use. Consequently, worm tubs were ruled out when the distillery was founded (every penny a prisoner at that stage). But after eight years' operation the new-style condensers were worn out.

What did he replace them with? Worm tubs, of course. And just so everyone understood what he'd done and why, Caldenby posted a near-800-word blog on the Smögen website. You've got to love that.

78

Distillery Spirit of Hven
Visitor Centre Backafallsbyn, Hven
Website Yes
www.backafallsbyn.se

Whisky	
Where	
When	
Verdict	

Spirit of Hven

What first sets this Swedish whisky apart is the very distinctive and unusual packaging. Resembling a laboratory flask, it comes as no surprise to learn that owner and founder Henric Molin is a trained chemist and also offers consulting services.

But there's more to this set-up than a funky bottle. Established in 2007 to create Swedish whisky, the Backafallsbyn distillery was Sweden's third-ever pot-still distillery, part of a wider movement there that has grown rapidly and is now well established. It's located on the tiny island of Hven, situated in the Öresund strait between Denmark and Sweden, which you can only reach by boat. With fewer than 350 inhabitants, think more of Jura than Islay.

And, like Islay, peated styles have proved something of a Swedish speciality. Hven's first release was the lightly peated Urania, and they've gone on to release the Seven Stars series of annual limited editions, a rye whisky and their own take on corn whisky, Mercurious, made largely from cereal grown in the distillery's own fields.

On top of that, they make rum, vodka, aquavit and a very respectable gin. Just as well then that they operate a resort hotel alongside their own restaurant and pub – tasting here could take a long time!

The most recent expression is called The Nose. No, it's not a reference to a well-known and flamboyant Scottish Master Blender but harks back to the famous astronomer Tycho Brahe (1546–1601) who was appointed Feudal Lord of Hven, though he didn't get on at all well with the locals. As a student Brahe had lost his nose in a duel with his third cousin, though he looks quite dapper in the gold prosthetic he's wearing on the label. Interesting guy, actually, and worth reading up on.

The whisky is pretty interesting also. Aged between 8 and 12 years, it matures in a complex blend of different types of casks using both French and American oak and a marriage stage in Spanish ex-oloroso sherry butts, after which it's bottled at 44.9% abv. In short, someone's gone to a lot of trouble here so not just for the bottle, you really should try to sniff one out.

Sweden

173

79

Distillery Käsers Schloss
Visitor Centre The Whisky Castle, Elfingen
Website Yes
www.kaesers-schloss.ch

Whisky	
Where	
When	
Verdict	

Käsers Schloss

Put away your cynicism. Forget the jokes about chocolate and cuckoo clocks. Don't dare mention *The Third Man*. Believe it or not, there are more than a dozen distilleries making whisky in Switzerland. You can be forgiven for not knowing about this, though, since firstly, they're all small and, secondly, whisky couldn't be distilled there legally until July 1999.

However, I was so sceptical that I went to visit one of the very first and best-known distilleries – The Whisky Castle at Elfingen – where they started making whisky almost immediately the law was changed. Like a number of small distillers, they made their first few batches in the stainless-steel still normally used for fruit schnapps (at which, incidentally, the Käser family excel). Being perfectionists, they weren't happy with the result, so they invested in a dedicated copper pot still – then unique in Switzerland.

Nothing had quite prepared me for the pure delight of the distillery itself, though, which has been constructed in the style of a traditional American Shaker barn, and also accommodates a small restaurant for pre-booked groups, a galleried bar and a dramatic picture window through to the warehouse. It is all thoroughly admirable.

This being a long-standing family business, Ruedi Käser, who first created the whisky, has stepped back since my visit and his two sons, Michael and Raphael, are in charge. Development hasn't stopped though and today the range includes the Family Reserve, Doublewood, Smoked Barley and a cream liqueur as well as the fruit brandies you'd expect to find here. They've also dropped the Whisky Castle name in favour of calling the business Käsers Schloss (it is a family concern after all) – a label change awaits.

The flagship expression is the Edition Käser, now bottled after 8 years of age maturation in a cask formerly used for Bordeaux wine and at a hard-hitting 65% abv. Most is, of course, sold in Switzerland, but supplies have been exported to Germany, The Netherlands, Austria and China. If you can't arrange a visit, the website offers online sales, though I keep hoping that some enterprising retailer will arrange to sell at least one of these whiskies in the UK. Swiss whisky: I'm pretty certain that would be a banker.

Switzerland

80

Distillery

Visitor Centre
Website

Langatun
Langatun, Eyhalde 10,
4912 Aarwangen
Yes
www.langatun.ch

Whisky

Where

When

Verdict

CLASSIC WHISKY

LANGATUN ✚
THE SWISS SINGLE MALT

OLD DEER

Langatun

There's a long and slightly tangled history of brewing and distilling here but the present-day story really started in the town of Langenthal in 2008 when the first whisky, The Olde Deer, was released. Distilling in earnest started shortly afterwards and, following several changes of ownership and expansion to a new site, the whisky was marketed internationally from 2017. Today Old Deer (it's lost its e somewhere) is distilled in the charming and historic Kornhaus in Aarwangen, roughly located between Zurich and Bern though still matured in the company's original Langenthal home.

They ship globally, but I thought I'd mention that UK distribution is handled by a former Glenfarclas marketing manager, an endorsement of some serious whisky credentials. The distillery are somewhat coy about their production methods, describing it as involving 'secret recipes and processes [that] are revealed to only a few select people'. Actually, don't let on but they use English stout yeast for fermentation (pretty hipster, that) and have been pioneering with their cask selection, the aim being to create wine-cask-matured whisky.

In a nod to the distillery's early years, Langatun Old Deer is the signature expression, employing unsmoked barley matured in Chardonnay and sherry casks. But they also offer a smoky whisky, imaginatively named Old Bear, which uses malt that's been wood-smoked rather than over peat, and matured in casks that previously held Châteauneuf du Pape, so very different from an Islay-style peated whisky. Both are bottled as NAS – so assume that they're not very old – at 46% abv, and are also available at cask strength. There are a number of special editions and limited releases available from time to time as well as gin, rum and a vodka so, considering the scale, the distillers have certainly not been idle!

But I suspect their heart lies in the Old Deer and it's certainly a rather charming and immediately appealing drop, loaded with fruit and floral aromas, sweet dark fruits and oak on the palate and some roasted nuts and spice to finish; altogether it's very well integrated and nicely balanced. A great advert for Swiss whisky, proof that the country's not all watches and chocolate – but read on to learn what devilment Seven Seals have planned.

Switzerland

177

81

Distillery
Visitor Centre
Website

Seven Seals
Langatun
No
www.7sealswhisky.com

Whisky	
Where	
When	
Verdict	

Seven Seals

I approached this bottle with some trepidation, for is it not foretold that the opening of the seventh seal marks the end of days? Well, brand names are generally chosen with great consideration for their deeper meaning so we may reasonably assume a blunt message was intended for someone.

Speeding up the aging process in spirits (unlike in writers, where it accelerates naturally) has long been something of the Holy Grail for some drinks companies. If you could obtain the same taste profile from six-month-old spirit as one that has spent ten years in wood, just consider the saving in casks and warehouses. Imagine the additional profits. Why, you might even be able to offer lower retail prices, though perhaps that's a trifle fanciful. But people have been trying for over a century (Dewar's tried in 1911) and, despite great experimentation, we aren't much further forward than the use of small barrel sizes and, more recently, STR casks. However, Seven Seals' entrepreneurial owner, scientist Dr Dolf Stockhausen, says he has the answer, which is (cue drumroll) $F/E \times C + Q = 7S$.

Further details are under wraps while the Swiss Federal Patent Office consider granting legal protection to Seven Seals' secret technique, but it's possible to deduce that it involves heat, aromatised wood particles and an understanding of Fick's Law of Diffusion* to accelerate the process of flavour development. So far, Seven Seals have been working with 3-year-old Langatun whiskies (see 80) as their base but have wider ambitions to license their technology.

Whatever your view, we can perhaps agree on one thing: their slogan 'Time doesn't matter, Taste matters'. After all, this is essentially what the Scotch whisky industry maintained with the so-called NAS releases a few years ago, largely as a result of stocks and demand getting out of balance. Except, major revelation, consumers didn't agree; there was pushback against NAS expressions and aged statements quickly reappeared. So, Frankenwhisky, or does accelerated maturation presage an apocalyptic future for established distillers? You and your wallet will choose.

Switzerland

---

* Which postulates that 'the rate of diffusion is proportional to both the surface area and concentration difference and is inversely proportional to the thickness of the membrane'.

82

Distillery Kavalan, Yuan Shan
Visitor Centre Yes
Website www.kavalanwhisky.com

Kavalan

Whisky	
Where	
When	
Verdict	

KA
VA
LAN

SINGLE MALT
WHISKY

Kavalan distillery select

Nº 1 | **DISTILLERY SELECT**
Delicate and silky. Full with the scent of tropical fruits, fragrant floral notes, and sweet vanilla.

40% vol. 700ml 70cl℮

Kavalan

Right now, Kavalan is world whisky's poster boy – a genuine new star in whisky's firmament, making whisky of exceptional quality. The Distillery Select is their entry level (and quite the bargain) but frankly, just buy anything you see without hesitation. The history of the distillery is, by Western standards, staggering. Observing the local passion for whisky, company Chairman T. T. Lee decided to build the distillery as recently as 2005. He flew his technical crew and R&D team to Scotland, hired the renowned Dr Jim Swan and started work. Fast.

Right from the start, this was an impressive operation combining the best of traditional techniques, with pot stills manufactured in Scotland, alongside innovative engineering and automation. After several phases of expansion it is today one of the largest single-malt distilleries anywhere in the world, able to make up to 10 million bottles annually – an astonishing achievement.

Next door is the huge visitor centre, which can host 24,000 visitors a week – more than a million annually; that's more than all of Scotland's visitor centres combined and a truly impressive achievement. The first whisky was released in 2008 and astonished experts. In blind tests for *The Times* of London a panel of experienced tasters placed it above a number of Scotch whiskies of a similar age and it has since won multiple international awards, continuing to surprise and delight with every new release.

The reason that such a young whisky performed so remarkably well is a combination of the distillery's design, great cask selection and the rapid speed of maturation in Taiwan's intense heat and humidity. Storage conditions create very high rates of evaporation and it's possible to bottle remarkably mature-tasting whisky in just three to four years, though the spirit is now proving to age very well. Kavalan have also pioneered the use of STR casks and released some quite superb expressions: if your budget will stretch, try something – anything – from their Solist range.

More recently, their popular Master Distiller Ian Chang has departed to run his own consultancy and lead a distilling team in Japan, but he has left a great legacy: if this is world whisky it's clear that Scotland and Kentucky have a fight on their hands.

Taiwan

83

Distillery Omar
Visitor Centre Nantou, Nantou City
Website Yes
www.omarwhisky.com.tw

Whisky	
Where	
When	
Verdict	

Omar

While Kavalan (see 82) really dominates Western perceptions of whisky from Taiwan it's worth noting that this whisky-mad island actually has two producers, though by contrast with its private-sector competitor the Nantou Distillery is government owned. In fact, the Taiwan and Tobacco & Liquor Corporation (TTL) had a complete monopoly on tobacco and alcohol until 2002. In 2008 construction of the Nantou Distillery began and two large pairs of Forsyths stills were installed. Malted barley is also imported from Scotland and, as related on the website, '. . . in order to reach excellence, selected craft man went to Scotland to study for making, distilling and maturing technology'.

No pretence is made to any great innovations in technique or product development, rather Nantou aims to marry traditional Scotch whisky technique, with local *terroir* and creativity, giving Taiwanese whisky its distinctive tropical fruit flavours. This is reflected in the somewhat limited product range available in export markets, comprising a core range of two single malts, aged in bourbon and sherry casks respectively; the Omar Cask Strength range and Omar Single Peated, using peat brought from Scotland, which has attracted positive reviews. The Liqueur Finish range employs wine or liqueur casks but quantities appear to be limited, with none currently seen in Europe.

In 2016, Omar Bourbon Cask and Omar Sherry Cask were launched in the UK but have made relatively little headway in a crowded market. Instead, the focus is on Taiwan itself and the company's export efforts seem to prioritise Japan, Korea and Russia. More recently, a blended malt called Yushan was developed and under the more premium Yushan Signature label two single-malt expressions, again either bourbon- or sherry-cask aged, have been launched. Unfortunately, few further details of casks or age are forthcoming. All the styles are mid-priced for their category and 20-cl bottles of Omar represent an opportunity to try this little-known whisky without a major financial commitment.

Nantou's relative anonymity in the West notwithstanding, something is clearly going right for their business as an expansion project has been announced, though once again details are sparse. Doubtless we shall be enlightened in due course, though Kavalan continues to set the pace.

Taiwan

84

Distillery | **Balcones**
Visitor Centre | Balcones, Waco, Texas
Website | Yes
| www.balconesdistilling.com

Whisky

Where

When

Verdict

BALCONES

BABY BLUE
made from roasted blue corn

750 ml   CORN WHISKY   46% alc./vol.

THE ORIGINAL ★ TEXAS WHISKY

Balcones

For a while back in 2013 and 2014, Balcones was the hottest thing on the US craft-distilling scene; beloved of bloggers, with a rapidly developing cult following amongst whisky's chattering classes who fell over themselves to heap praise on some single-minded and innovative products and the charismatic founder, Chip Tate. But 'pride comes before a fall', or 'walk before you can run' or some such similarly sententious sentiment. Not long after that everything imploded: Tate had a spectacularly acrimonious public falling out with his backers and left to set up again on his own. Presumably he and his avid fans assumed Balcones would then fold ignominiously.

Far from it: 'no one is irreplaceable' and life carried on under head distiller Jared Himstedt who had been with Balcones since its inception. In fact, things got better (well, larger) as the distillery moved to a new 6,000-square-metre site in downtown Waco – close to the original distillery – with some shiny new stills from Forsyths. It's capable of an impressive 350,000 litres annually, but then as the natives are wont to remind us, Texas is a big place.

Today Balcones have several core-range products: Texas '1' Single Malt, Brimstone, Baby Blue, True Blue, Lineage, Texas Rye, Pot Still Bourbon, plus a number of limited editions such as Rumble Cask Reserve and distillery-only special releases. As many more small distilleries have opened up across the USA some of the intensity of interest in Balcones has diminished, but my impression is of a company and brands maturing nicely into its second decade of operations.

Baby Blue was their first product and, in fact, the first legally distilled whisky in Texas since Prohibition. It's also the only whisky (yes, that's how they spell it) made from Hopi blue corn, a strikingly vivid blue American Indian heirloom flint corn used in traditional Southern and central Mexican cuisine. It's certainly an appealing drop and one perhaps to compare with Abasolo (see 54).

I asked my wife to try some and she reacted as follows: 'That's whisky with all the unpleasant bits taken out.' As all the unpleasantness at Balcones is behind them and all is now sweet harmony, you can't really say fairer than that.

85

Distillery

Visitor Centre
Website

Catoctin Creek
Catoctin Creek, Purcellville, Virginia
Yes
www.catoctincreekdistilling.com

Whisky	
Where	
When	
Verdict	

Catoctin Creek

I appreciate that by now you've probably read about quite a number of rye whiskies. Well, bear with me because we're nearly there and this is a good one. No, make that a *great* one. A US buddy, Scott Schiller, put me onto this. As his business is helping small craft distilleries get started and grow I promised him a name check. Hi, Scott.

One of the reasons rye is so important is that it's the original style of American whiskey, with the first documentation dating back to 1640 when William Kieft, director of the Dutch colony of New Amsterdam (that's roughly the Battery Park and Wall Street area of Manhattan), ordered rye to be distilled.

As it grew in popularity, it spread down into Pennsylvania, Maryland and Virginia where we find Catoctin Creek. President George Washington was making rye at Mount Vernon,* about 60 miles from Catoctin Creek, back in the 1790s at which time there were probably more than 3,600 distilleries in the state of Virginia alone. But after Prohibition rye lost out to bourbon (and, sad to say, vodka and white rum) and by the 1980s was a pale shadow of its former self. However, it has staged a major comeback in recent years and is now greatly appreciated.

That's thanks in no small measure to distilleries such as Catoctin Creek which was founded by Becky and Scott Harris in 2009 as the first legal distillery in Loudoun County since before Prohibition. The name derives from the Indian tribal name Kittocton and describes a range of mountains and the eponymous creek which flows past the distillery, into the Potomac River and on down to Washington DC .

Here they make gin (who doesn't these days) and various fruit brandies but their flagship product is the highly awarded Roundstone Rye, made with an eye to replicating old-world production. There are three options: the original 80 proof (40% abv) version; a 46% abv Distiller's Edition and the full-on Cask Proof, around 58% abv, which they release twice a year. A pre-Prohibition style, Roundstone is made from 100 per cent rye grain and mashed, fermented, distilled and aged completely at the distillery. Whichever you can track down, Catoctin Creek is not to be missed.

USA

86

Distillery
Visitor Centre
Website

Cleveland
Cleveland, Ohio
Yes
www.clevelandwhiskey.com

Whisky	
Where	
When	
Verdict	

Cleveland

And now, as they used to say, for something completely different. Well, not completely different, but a little bit off-beat. It's another attempt at accelerated maturation – also found at Seven Seals (see 81), the Lost Spirits Distillery in Los Angeles, and Bespoken Spirits – as various entrepreneurs use the appliance of science to overturn both the traditions and orthodoxy of conventional whisky aging.

The industry establishment's PR machine holds that 60 per cent (or sometimes more) of a whisky's final flavour is derived from the barrel, hence all the various finishes that are offered and the importance attached to detailing the cask in which said whisky has been aged throughout every stage in its life. It's also stressed that this process cannot be rushed, something enshrined in the many laws surrounding whisky's production and labelling. If nothing else, this gives people like me something to write about and whisky bores a rich source of trivia to mine and then argue over (any correlation between these two categories is entirely coincidental).

But it has also caused a number of iconoclastic would-be malt magnates to question the whole basis of aging, spotting the profit opportunity in subverting current practice by accelerating the aging process and experimenting with different woods. Oak has long been the preferred choice for barrel construction because its close, straight grain allows it to be formed into staves that are virtually leak proof. (Alcohol hasn't always been stored in oak casks. Roman wine went into large European silver fir barrels and research suggests they worked just fine.) It follows that if the barrel can be replaced then other woods can be used and the flavours they offer explored.

Cleveland, established in 2013 and now operating from their own distillery, take very young whiskey with fewer than six months, conventional maturation, put it in pressurised stainless steel tanks along with small pieces of the selected wood (they call them BRICX™ and sell the used blocks as barbecue fuel), which is then exposed to changes in pressure, temperature and oxygenation. Their Underground Bourbon employs hickory and black cherry wood to introduce new and unexpected flavours to the spirit.

Web reviews, it has to be said, tend to the snide and critical (of course, that could just be the web for you). For my part, I'm inclined to wait and see if Cleveland have added something worthwhile; only time will tell – which is the point of aging, after all.

USA

87

Distillery | **Corsair**
Corsair Artisan Distillery,
Nashville, Tennessee
Visitor Centre | Yes
Website | www.corsairartisan.com

Whisky	
Where	
When	
Verdict	

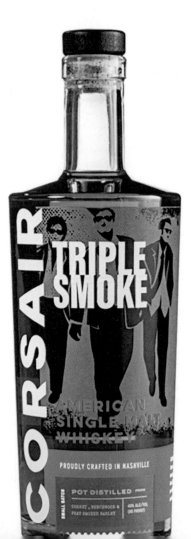

Corsair

Once upon a time Corsair (it means 'privateer' or 'pirate' – a name they didn't pick by accident) Artisan (we know what that means, again not idly chosen) claimed to make small-batch 'ultra-premium booze for Badasses'. But having spent $11 million in 2018 to expand in Nashville, they seemed to have calmed down somewhat and gone just a little bit corporate. Can't blame them. $11 million is a lot of spondulicks.

But the *Reservoir Dogs* style label remains (they use variations of it on almost everything), suggesting that there's a certain consciously iconoclastic attitude in their DNA. It's not some surly, adolescent snarling however; behind the pose there is a well-thought-out appeal to the market and a deep commitment to experimentation and innovation in distilled spirits. They make red absinthe for goodness' sake.

Probably best known here for their gin, they've been going since early 2008, when Corsair fairly rapidly found favour with opinion formers in the cocktail-bar community. Along the way they've collected more than 800 awards, though as the list includes quite a few Bronze awards from essentially regional competitions they might seem to be shouting just a little too loudly (he suggested, with typically English diffidence). Maybe just tell us about the big ones, of which to be fair they have more than a few.

As well as counting medals and making some money, founders Darek Bell and Andrew Webber, have made a mark on the spirits business with Bell's book, *Alt Whiskeys*, a major influence on others in the craft-distilling community. So, as you'd expect, they make some unusual whiskeys: Quinoa, Citra Double IPA Hopped, Pumpkin Spiced Moonshine, Wry Moon American Rye Spirit and a bewildering variety of other expressions, often in limited runs. It's hard to keep up, to be honest, and not easy to find the more esoteric releases outside the USA.

However, the Wry Moon, made with an antique wash still and Corsair's handmade pot still, does crop up on several UK websites and, loving a pun as much as the next man, I mention it here as representative of their range. Their approach has brought us unusual whiskeys at sensible prices. Churlish, really, to ask for more.

USA

88

Distillery	**Frey Ranch**
Visitor Centre	Frey Ranch, Fallon, Nevada
Website	Yes
	www.freyranch.com

Whisky	
Where	
When	
Verdict	

Frey Ranch

'Be good to the land and the land will be good to you,' says Colby Frey, who styles himself 'Farmer + Distiller' and is to be found working on a 'whiskey farm'. And this is truly a farm-to-glass enterprise that takes distilling back to its roots in agriculture. With every drop derived from grains grown, malted, distilled, matured, and bottled all on the 2,500-acre Frey family ranch based in the Lake Tahoe watershed of the Sierra Nevada, this is not your typical bourbon location, and all the better for that. The family have been here since 1854 apparently, so this doesn't feel like an overly hasty decision to jump on the craft-distilling bandwagon.

Once Nevada had approved regulations for small-scale distilling in 2010, planning could begin in earnest and the Frey Ranch distillery officially launched in 2014. Using an impressive Vendome column still (from the Rolls Royce of US still makers) Frey is clearly well funded, something else reflected in the imposing packaging and, more importantly, the admirable decision to age the bourbon a full four years prior to release.

It's garnered impressive plaudits from US reviewers, greatly taken with the four-grain mash bill – two-thirds non-GMO corn, and around 10 per cent each of winter cereal rye, winter wheat and two-row barley. The inclusion of the rye definitely contributes a distinctively spicy and drying note to counter the corn's sugarcane sweetness and overall this presents as a very nicely balanced whiskey, drinking well at the 45% abv bottling strength.

For a relatively new operation it's an impressive debut, with a whiskey that retains sufficient body to stand up well in cocktails. Armed with that justifiable confidence, Frey Ranch also offer a single-barrel variant, alongside vodka, gin, absinthe (which retains something of a cult following as a style in the USA) and a rye whiskey, which gets an extra year of barrel age.

Frey Ranch was initially only available in Nevada and northern California but its fame spread quickly, and as we go to press plans are apparently well advanced to bring stock to the UK where I expect it to receive a warm welcome.

USA

89

Distillery	**High West**
Visitor Centre	MGP Ingredients, Indiana
Website	Yes
	www.highwest.com

Whisky	
Where	
When	
Verdict	

High West

Here's a whiskey that's not been without its share of controversy. Though bottled under the High West label, this wasn't actually distilled there – but it is very good and has made the reputation of the High West operation, now distilling its own whiskeys on two different sites in Park City, Utah.

Proprietor David Perkins and his wife established High West, Utah's first licensed distillery for nearly 140 years, in 2007 and immediately began small-scale distilling. They also started bottling rye whiskies such as the Rendezvous Rye. Despite initially facing criticism that the source – the giant MGP Ingredients distillery in Lawrenceburg, Indiana – wasn't immediately apparent, the quality soon won over the critics and further releases followed. Indeed, a number of other companies have successfully sourced and bottled fine whiskies made by MGP and the practice has become more widely accepted. Moreover, the sensitive architectural restoration of the historic buildings of High West's Utah home placated critics by demonstrating that the distillery was in good, thoughtful hands with a view to the long term.

High West substantially expanded distilling in 2015 and now release a number of their own whiskeys such as the American Prairie Bourbon. In October 2016 the business and brands were acquired by Constellation Brands, a major American distillery group, in a rumoured $160-million takeover, said to have been contested by Pernod Ricard and LVMH (owners of Glenmorangie). So arguably, it's no longer 'craft' and it certainly isn't independent.

But despite that, I'm sticking with Rendezvous as the starting point to explore High West. Unlike lesser ryes, here you can experience a dramatically high rye content delivering a very traditional style, well aged with full-on flavour delivery and 46% abv bottling strength that initially takes your breath away – and, if you don't know the style, will cause you to rethink this American blue-collar classic.

It's little surprise that it's been so well received in competitions and quickly won many fans amongst top mixologists. Rendezvous was a significant contributor to the renaissance of rye whiskey and for that reason maintains an honoured place here. Well done MGP Ingredients for making this, and well done High West for plucking it from their warehouses and bringing it to the world!

USA

90

Distillery

Visitor Centre
Website

Hudson
Tuthilltown, Gardiner,
New York State
Yes
www.hudsonwhiskey.com

Whisky	
Where	
When	
Verdict	

Hudson

Like a number of their US counterparts, Hudson is now part of a larger group – in this case, Scotland's William Grant & Sons. Their arrival on the craft-distilling scene was quite the phenomenon though and for a while, less than 15 years ago (an incredible length of time, given how whisky has developed, but writing this makes me feel very old), Hudson was the hottest thing on the trendy cocktail-bar scene. The coolest mixologists in town were fighting to get hold of a 37.5-cl bottle of Baby Bourbon at around £100; pretty fancy pricing for a tiny operation that only started distilling whiskey in 2006 but immediately collected any number of top awards and inspired numerous imitators.

What's particularly amusing is that Ralph Erenzo, who with business partner Brian Lee founded the distillery, originally planned to start a climbing centre on an old farm site. That met stiff opposition from the locals but a lucky conversation with a planning officer revealed that an agriculture-based project could not be refused permission – and so the idea of a distillery, the first in the state since Prohibition, was born. Probably not what the nimby lobby had in mind.

Then, more good fortune: in June 2010 William Grant & Sons acquired the Hudson whiskey brands (though not at that time the distillery) and took over their worldwide distribution, presenting the opportunity for the brand's international breakthrough. Their cash enabled the distillery to expand, meaning that it became available in standard-sized bottles and prices dropped somewhat as production was expanded. Grant's full takeover followed in April 2017.

The distillery itself, in the beautiful Hudson Valley, is a delight to visit, especially as it represents a breakthrough in US craft distilling. It's well worth the trip from the Big Apple for the scenery alone and the chance to sample a flight of all their spirits.

They also make several tasty ryes but as bourbon made their name I'll stick with this grown-up baby – rebranded as Bright Lights, Big Bourbon and in a larger bottle, it's 95% corn with 5% malted barley for a bold, no-holds-barred straight bourbon whiskey.

USA

91

Distillery	**Jeptha Creed** Jeptha Creed, Shelbyville, Kentucky
Visitor Centre	Yes
Website	www.jepthacreed.com

Whisky	
Where	
When	
Verdict	

Jeptha Creed

I'd like to imagine an old-time Jeptha once distilling here in real life but, more prosaically, the name comes from the Jeptha Knob, a local geological landmark. But that could have led to some confusion and even ribaldry so this new craft distillery has adopted a creed to stress its commitment to local production, with as many ingredients as possible coming from the family's or their neighbours' farms.

Unusually, it's a mother-and-daughter operation though here again they strike a traditional note as, going back far enough, distilling was predominantly a female occupation while menfolk took on the heavier farm work (and huntin' and shootin' and all the fun stuff). The Nethery family have been here since the 1700s and, inspired to create their own distilling tradition, mother and daughter Joyce and Autumn Nethery are the powerhouses behind Jeptha Creed.

Master Distiller Joyce actually worked as an engineer for a much larger distiller prior to a decade in science education, and daughter Autumn, who manages marketing, studied at Edinburgh's Heriot-Watt University. They've come together to deliver a vision of a 'ground to glass' operation that, in August 2016, distilled and filled the first legal barrel of bourbon in Shelby County since before Prohibition – remarkable considering that in around 30 miles on Highway 64 you're in the centre of Louisville.

They make a variety of spirits but the smooth and easy-drinking Straight Four Grain Bourbon is the standout, with its heritage corn-heavy mash bill featuring 70 per cent Bloody Butcher Corn; 15 per cent malted rye; 10 per cent malted wheat and 5 per cent malted barley.

Two things to note: the inclusion of malted cereals was pure serendipity; due to some confusion in trials malted grains were supplied, but once tried were immediately included in the final recipe. And Bloody Butcher, so prominent on the label, refers to a heirloom varietal grown on the Nethery farm that has proved highly successful in whiskey.

It's still a small-batch operation, with just nine barrels made each day. Refreshingly in a world where too many small operators are focused on their exit route and waiting for the call from a larger rival, the Netherys plan to keep this in the family – it's their creed.

USA

92

Distillery   Koval
Visitor Centre   Koval, Chicago, Illinois
Website   Yes
   www.koval-distillery.com

Whisky

Where

When

Verdict

KOVAL

SINGLE BARREL
WHISKEY

Millet

DISTILLED IN CHICAGO

40% vol 500ML

Koval

What's whisky made from? Easy: barley, corn, rye and wheat. Custom, practice and legislation have led to the global dominance of these four cereals, and with the many wonderful whiskies that are created from them, we don't need to look any further.

Well, apparently, we do and a new generation of distillers are asking, 'What about oats, or millet?'

At the leading edge of this new wave enquiring into the characteristics of unorthodox grains is this independent, family-owned Chicago distillery, established in 2008 by Drs Robert and Sonat Birnecker, a husband-and-wife team who chose to leave academic careers to bring the distilling traditions of Robert's Austrian family to America. Right from the start they made the decision to do things differently: using only organic, non-GMO grains; taking only the 'heart' cut of the distillate for their whiskey and bottling everything as single-barrel expressions, employing small (113.5-litre) barrels with full traceability from bottle to individual barrel to the specific farm that provided the raw material. Not that uncommon these days, though few carry the pursuit of transparency to quite this obsessive degree, but very unusual and pioneering back in 2008, especially as the Birneckers had funded their early development by juggling their credit-card limits. (NB: Don't try this at home.)

They make quite a range of spirits: liqueurs, peach and prune brandy, vodka, gin and a number of whiskeys. Some are what you'd expect: Bourbon and Rye feature, alongside a tasty-sounding Four Grain. But look closer and there's something unexpected, namely the Oat and Millet whiskeys. That latter grain is highly unorthodox in distilling, though millet is hugely important as a food source in much of Asia and Africa. It's also gluten free which might explain its appeal to Western millennials, though Koval don't make any such health claim, confiding only that it offers a 'truly singular drinking experience'.

Having kick-started the craft-distilling movement in Chicago and lobbied successfully for changes to local laws blocking tasting rooms and direct-to-consumer sales, and with their pioneering attitude and 'why not' approach, Koval have been an inspiration and role model for other small distillers. Great value and great products. Who can ask for more?

USA

93

Distillery | **New Riff**
Visitor Centre | New Riff, Newport, Kentucky
Website | Yes
| www.newriffdistilling.com

Whisky	
Where	
When	
Verdict	

New Riff

It takes a certain confidence and independence of mind to suggest that you're doing something new and different in a field as long established and with so many traditions and well-regarded competitors as whiskey. Calling yourself New Riff and proclaiming your 'transparency' across your website does rather raise the stakes and, in an interesting demonstration of architecture as metaphor, constructing a glass tower to house your column still is a powerful demonstration of openness. (Mind you, Scottish architect George Darge was employing glass curtain walls on the still houses of many DCL distilleries in the 1970s, and more recently both Dalmunach and The Macallan have made extensive use of glass walling.)

So good for the defiantly independently owned New Riff, making their bourbon, rye and other spirits in Newport, on the border of Kentucky and Ohio. The commitment here to independent ownership, tradition blended with innovation and proper aging of the spirits is overt, unambiguous and loudly public.

They've gone for a mash bill of non-GMO grains at 65 per cent corn, 30 per cent rye, and 5 per cent malted barley, resulting in a teasing, spicy character which, combined with a 50 per cent bottling strength, is certainly uncompromising. More importantly for purists, New Riff lay great stress on their strict adherence to full sour mash Kentucky Regimen and insist, just a trifle defensively I feel, that 'not only is this Kentucky's unique whiskey tradition, but it's also a fantastic way to make any whiskey, every bit as good as the processes of Scotland and elsewhere'. I don't think anyone seriously doubts that and it's been many, many years since anyone could maintain that Scotch holds a monopoly on the distilling of fine whisky (for one thing, it would make this book somewhat pointless if that were so).

Unusually, though, New Riff is 'bottled in bond' which is, in effect, a consumer-protection guarantee dating back to the late 1890s that ensures the origin, strength and age of the whiskey. That's New Riff distancing themselves from the practice of buying spirit from another distiller and marketing it as the purchaser's brand, something which was regrettably commonplace in the recent explosion of interest in craft distilling.

So, to be clear, they may be riffing but definitely not improvising.

USA

94

Distillery	**Peerless**
	Kentucky Peerless, Louisville, Kentucky
Visitor Centre	Yes
Website	www.kentuckypeerless.com

Whisky	
Where	
When	
Verdict	

Peerless

Having noted New Riff's irreverent stance (see 93) it takes a certain chutzpah to declare your distillery 'Peerless' (i.e. 'without equal') and set up shop right in the heart of Louisville, the world capital of bourbon. Right along the street you can find Michter's Fort Nelson Distillery and the Evan Williams Bourbon Experience; just down the block the Frazier History Museum is home to the Kentucky Bourbon Trail Welcome Center and the official starting point of the Kentucky Bourbon Trail. This is Bourbon Central.

So what's an upstart little distillery, opened as recently as 2015, doing in this exalted company? Well, there's a hint in the cryptic legend on the front of the distillery, reading DSP-KY-50. It's a link to distilling heritage, being the original Kentucky Distilled Spirits Plant Number from the Taylor family's historical ownership of the first Peerless distillery, which, like so many others, was a casualty of Prohibition, closing around a hundred years ago.

It's the equivalent, I suppose, of putting a vintage registration plate on a modern car because at the same time Peerless make great play of this remembrance of times past we're told that the current operation is 'a state-of-the-art facility with cutting-edge technology, making it one of the most automated distilleries'. I guess you can have it all.

But that's marketing for you. Leaving that aside, Peerless have been attracting quite a number of favourable reviews for the quality of their rye and bourbon whiskeys, though social media was less enamoured of the launch pricing. Notwithstanding that, the highly influential *Whisky Advocate* magazine declared it to be their top rye in 2017 and again in 2018 – no mean accolade for a two-year-old product from a small start-up operation led by a new, young Master Distiller with little previous industry experience (but then he's running a highly automated distillery).

I have to mention the bottle, because the owning family take great pride on the website in explaining how they designed it, how it's very heavy with a substantial and weighty cork stamped with that DSP-KY-50 and how it sits on a plinth and so on and so forth. So, if you didn't know before, now you do. Just don't drop it on your foot.

USA

95

Distillery	**Reservoir** Reservoir Distillery, Richmond, Virginia
Visitor Centre	Yes
Website	www.reservoirdistillery.com

Whisky	
Where	
When	
Verdict	

Reservoir

By now you will have noticed there are no detailed tasting notes here and certainly no scores. As previously explained, that's because you know what you like, can afford and already have in your drinks cabinet much better than I do and, to the extent that I have a philosophy, it's that whisky is for everyone to explore and enjoy without my didactic pontifications (or, indeed, those of any other 'expert'). So I was delighted to see this on the Reservoir Distillery's website: 'We believe in "creating your own tradition", honoring the fact that everyone has a unique palate.' Amen! It's almost as if they'd read this book.

So in that spirit I point you towards this single-minded Virginia distillery, established in 2008 by childhood friends Jay Carpenter and Dave Cuttino. They only make single-grain whiskeys. The Bourbon Whiskey is 100 per cent corn, the Rye Whiskey is 100 per cent rye. And, as you've probably guessed by now, the Wheat Whiskey is 100 per cent wheat.

All of those grains come from within 50 miles of the distillery and they age in 13-gallon casks (US gallons that is, so just less than 11 imperial gallons) that they use only once and which have received a custom alligator char. That's pretty much as deep as charring goes – Ardbeg did this in 2011 and, believe me, you don't want to know what a bottle of that would cost today.

I also like the suggestion that you blend to your own taste: buy a bottle of each of their whiskeys and create your own personal blend. It's not difficult and the worst that can happen is that you don't like it. In which case, put in a drop more of your favourite and see what happens. Then splash out on your own cask (they're available in a range of sizes) and try extra aging. Before you know it you're your own Master Blender and you discover you have many new friends. You might even start a business.

They also employed a local mural artist to paint the front of their distillery, presenting a fresh and vibrant face to the world. Apart from being exceptionally cool it struck me as an excellent metaphor for their entire *weltanschauung*. This reservoir is deep.

96

Distillery	**St. George's**
	St. George's Spirits, Alameda, California
Visitor Centre	Yes
Website	www.stgeorgespirits.com

Whisky	
Where	
When	
Verdict	

St. George's

Before there was craft distilling there was the St. George's Spirits distillery. Based in Alameda, California, this hugely influential operation is arguably the birthplace of the modern American artisan distillation movement. The business was founded in 1982 by Jörg Rupf, a German immigrant with family connections to the distilling of fruit spirits in the Black Forest. Aiming to re-create the *eaux de vie* styles he remembered from Germany, he established a small distillery and, in the process, changed everything that was then known about distilling in the USA.

Several other very well-known artisan distillers in the USA trained here and have gone on to establish their own operations, often with considerable success, and in consequence St. George's holds a special place in the industry's history. And St. George's, now owned by Lance Winters who joined Rupf in 1996, has grown to the point where it now occupies a 6,000-square-metre building and operates a number of stills, making a full range of spirits including distinctive and innovative American whiskeys and single malt.

Today whisky production is the responsibility of Dave Smith who together with Winters created the Baller Single Malt Whiskey – so called because it was created with Japanese-style whiskey highballs in mind. They describe it as 'A California take on the Japanese spin on Scotch whisky' – a sort of a fusion whisky one might say. It's typical of their experimental attitude and restless curiosity. Starting with American barley, the whiskey is aged in ex-bourbon casks and French oak wine casks, and then filtered through maple charcoal. The Japanese influence comes from finishing in casks that had held St. George's house-made *umeshu* (a plum liqueur they make entirely from California-grown ume fruit, though confusingly the ume is actually an apricot). Strange fruit.

The label is a further cultural mash-up. England's patron saint appears as a samurai in a watercolour illustration styled as a *ukiyo-e* woodblock print, complete with elegant *kanji* calligraphy. But like the whiskey it graces, there's a lot going on here. Served neat or in cocktails as intended, Baller is understandably not inexpensive but rewards mindful drinking with a delivery as distinctive and distinguished as the distillery's pedigree.

USA

97

Distillery Sonoma
Visitor Centre Yes
Website www.sonomadistillingcompany.com

Sonoma, Rohnert Park, California

Whisky	
Where	
When	
Verdict	

— PREMIUM CALIFORNIA WHISKEYS —

SONOMA
DISTILLING CO.

CHERRYWOOD RYE WHISKEY

80% RYE (CALIFORNIA & CANADA), 10% WHEAT (CALIFORNIA &
10% CHERRYWOOD SMOKED MALTED BARLEY

CALLY DOUBLE POT DISTILLED IN SONOMA COUNTY, CALIF

Sonoma

Distillers as they proudly claim of '100% Californian whiskey', Sonoma have since 2010 produced some remarkable products – a collaboration with Bow's East London Distillery; a cognac-barrel-finished wheat whiskey and the world's first black-truffle rye ('French Black Perigord truffles are steeped in spicy rye whiskey to create a spirit with a rich and creamy texture and notes of dates, mushrooms and honey'). I'm not sure there was enormous and frenzied competition to produce the world's first truffle-infused rye but it's certainly a striking proposition.

The Sonoma region brings wine production to mind and early visits to wine country planted the seed for founder Adam Spiegel, a refugee from the world of finance, to base his distillery here, becoming one of the earliest craft distilleries in California. I'm quite taken by this statement of intent from their website, even if the dreaded p-word has crept in. 'There are no "Masters" here per se; we're just passionate, talented, hard-working people striving every day to better ourselves and our craft. I like to say that we're making whiskeys in a small way, for a big world.' There's an appealing modesty and self-effacement about that in a world of aggrandisement and PR-driven hyperbole that appeals to my usually well-hidden inner Presbyterian. Let the whiskeys speak for themselves.

Their range is also tight; itself an encouraging sign that they aim to do a few things well, rather than dazzle us with an extravagant assortment of experiments. The Cherrywood Rye is something of an outlier though, combining Californian rye with a 10 per cent measure of state-grown wheat and cherrywood-smoked barley from Wyoming. The spirit is aged in a mix of 15-, 30- and 53-gallon new American oak barrels and the final product blended from these.

That and the Cherrywood-smoked barley marks this out from run-of-the-mill ryes, and when one learns that the product aims to emulate a Manhattan cocktail the unusual wood smoking starts to make sense. So much so in fact, that Sonoma also offer a cherrywood-smoked version of their Bourbon and have been successful in bringing these products to markets outside the USA despite the distillery's relatively modest scale.

98

Distillery

Visitor Centre
Website

Uncle Nearest
Nearest Green, Shelbyville,
Tennessee
Yes
www.unclenearest.com

Whisky	
Where	
When	
Verdict	

Uncle Nearest

Here's an unusual and cheering story. The original Nathan 'Nearest' Green was a black slave who most likely taught Jack Daniel how to distil. That's Jack Daniel's, as in the bestselling American whiskey in the world. But for years Green's contribution, and indeed that of other persons of colour, was little known.

That all changed in 2016 when writer and entrepreneur Fawn Weaver got interested in the story. As in, really, really interested, which ended up with her buying the original property where Green and Daniel started distilling. And then she launched a whiskey brand and, with help from both the Daniel and Green family, recruited an all-female executive team (including the whiskey maker and Master Blender) and an all-minority executive board to run the distillery they built. That's really unusual; though many more women have come to the fore in recent years, the distilling industry is not known for female senior management teams and the BAME community is undeniably under-represented.

Now Weaver has partnered with Brown-Forman, current owners of the Jack Daniel's brand, to launch a charitable foundation that will support African-American spirits entrepreneurs and offer apprenticeships to African-Americans seeking a production career in the industry.

The Uncle Nearest 1856 Premium Whiskey they have launched wasn't actually distilled at the Nearest Green distillery (which for one thing hadn't yet been built) but was an immediate success, becoming the fastest-growing independent premium American whiskey brand in US history and reaching over 100,000 cases sold annually in less than three years, despite the challenges of Covid and import tariffs that have restricted growth in the EU. The Nearest Green distillery didn't start production until autumn 2019 so it will be some while before their own whiskey reaches the market. Until then we'll have the contract-distilled product, which is sourced from two distilleries in Columbia, Tennessee, including Tennessee Distilling Group. Using a combination of corn and rye, the whiskeys are put through a unique coconut-shell charcoal filtration before being aged in new American oak barrels.

Judging by the awards it has already collected, Nathan Green's legacy is in careful hands and his important contribution to whiskey's history has at last been fully acknowledged.

USA

99

Distillery	**Westland**
	Westland, Seattle
Visitor Centre	Yes
Website	www.westlanddistillery.com

Whisky	
Where	
When	
Verdict	

Westland

Founded as recently as 2010, Westland is definitely a leader in American single malt and at the same time another craft distiller which has succumbed to the blandishments of a larger company. In this case, the ultimate owner is Rémy Cointreau who, to be fair, have proved to be benevolent owners of Bruichladdich. But, my goodness, just like the folks on Islay, Westland take themselves seriously – every painstaking detail to delight a whisky geek's heart is to be found on their website. If you wanted to know the temperature of their strike water – and who wouldn't – it's here.

It can get a trifle worthy. The opening video, full of grandiose aerial shots of sweeping landscapes and mighty forests, is laden with a sententious narrator delivering a virtue-signalling script dripping with every current PR cliché designed to appeal to the woke. I'm afraid it had this cynical Brit biting the keyboard as I tried, not terribly successfully, to contain my bitter laughter.

But clearly it works. Not only have the owners trousered a humongous pile of dollars but enthusiast consumers love it: I had to elbow my way through an increasingly frantic crowd at a recent whisky show in order to get to the stand for a prearranged meeting and then avoid their envious eyes as I departed with some modest samples. Mind you, one of the tiny bottles was of Westland's Garryana Oak American Single Malt which retails at around £165, so my fingers were wrapped round about 30-quid's worth.

However, this is interesting, pioneering whiskey that is asking questions of the old order and forging a new tradition. Around 170 distilleries are now distilling American single malt and Garryana reflects Westland's work with the rare indigenous Garryana oak: planting new trees and working to restore the health and diversity of the environment in which this once-threatened native species is found.

It's not necessary to break the bank though, as from the distillery's quite extensive range of limited editions, the flagship American Oak is freely available with Sherry Wood or Peated variants if you prefer.

Taste them and you'll understand why Rémy got their cheque book out.

USA

100

Distillery | **Penderyn**
Penderyn, Brecon Beacons
National Park
Visitor Centre | Yes
Website | www.penderyn.wales

Whisky	
Where	
When	
Verdict	

Penderyn

Time for some humble pie, I think, because I wasn't greatly impressed with the first Penderyns that I tasted when the distillery launched in 2004. I felt then that they were released too early and I was sceptical about Welsh whisky, thinking it something of a gimmick or tourist operation. Just shows you how wrong you can be, because this is a perfectly serious operation now exporting to more than 40 countries around the world.

However, part of my doubt arose as I wasn't convinced that the whisky still needed to be re-invented – Penderyn make much of their own unique design, termed the Faraday still, which produces spirit at around 92% abv, as opposed to the 60%-odd which would be normal in Scotland. This, they say, removes certain impurities that traditional pot stills leave behind. That's true. But it's also true to say that these impurities contribute flavour. Now Penderyn doesn't lack flavour, so how do they do it?

The main contributor is their wood regime where, as so often, the late Dr Jim Swan's influence may be detected as he was an adviser in the distillery's early days. For this Madeira finish, which is the original house style, the spirit starts off in ex-bourbon barrels (normal enough) and, in this case, is then finished in former Madeira drums. In total, it spends around five years in cask, the final year of which is in the Madeira wood. It is then reduced to 46% abv for bottling.

Like most of the small and new distilleries in this book, there are lots of different releases in the market including peated and sherry-wood styles, limited editions and single-cask bottlings, and several commemorating historic Welsh Grand Slam triumphs in rugby. Alternatively, you could try the distillery visitor centre where there is truly a welcome in the hillside and get the very latest bottlings.

Since opening, Penderyn has expanded, added a second Faraday still as well as some conventional Scottish stills. A second distillery is due to be opened in the Old Board House in Llandudno in 2021, with plans for a third, backed by a Heritage Lottery grant, in the historic Copper Quarter in Swansea, a couple of years later.

But, best of all, since 2015 they have sponsored a writers' prize for books about music. In this land of song and Dylan Thomas, what could be more appropriate?

Wales

101

Distillery

Visitor Centre
Website

World Whisky Blend
That Boutique-y Whisky Company
Planet Earth, The Universe, Outer Space
No
www.thatboutiqueywhiskycompany.com

Whisky	
Where	
When	
Verdict	

World Whisky Blend

This, according to the so-embarrassingly-bad-it's-good label, comprises 'a blend of incredible whiskies from Planet Earth'. It's from That Boutique-y Whisky Company, a part of Atom Brands' Master of Malt empire.

Now those various businesses do a lot of bottling of a lot of different casks of whisky so you might, if you were of an uncharitable turn of mind, suspect that they just take the various leftovers and mix them all together. Indeed, in this bottle you'll find whiskies from Scotland, Canada, Ireland, Sweden, USA, Switzerland, Netherlands, Taiwan, India, Italy, Germany, France, Japan and Finland. That's a lot of countries.

You might look upon that with great disdain, regarding it as an offence against whisky, or you could just note that it's as cheap as chips and think well, what's the harm. It's only a bit of fun. And it's not actually a completely new idea. Whisky 101 in the previous edition of this book was something called Orbis Aged World Whiskey that was aimed at a male international business traveller who (in the words of the brand, so don't blame me) 'has a global outlook, is confident, cosmopolitan, broad-minded'. Imagine being sat next to that smug git for hours on a plane. Anyway, despite being quite drinkable, it appears to have flopped.

Its disappearance hasn't put off the Boutique-y blending team, which is led by the company's Head of Whisky Dr Sam Simmons, a former brand ambassador for Balvenie, English Lit PhD and self-confessed whisky geek. What he's created here is more, I think, than a bit of fun. Though it's unlikely to ever be your all-time favourite whisky it works really, really well as a cocktail base. The World Whisky Blend has been designed for mixing which, after all, is how most of the world drinks most of its whisky. Try it, as they suggest, with green tea, coconut water, soda, ginger ale or, at a push, tonic.

They also mention cola but just don't. I'm as confident and broad-minded as the next international business traveller but there are limits.

All in order at Reisetbauer, Kirchdorfergut, Austria.

Acknowledgements

The biggest thanks go to all the distillers, all round the world, whose energy, enthusiasm and entrepreneurial spirit has made this book possible. And to you, whisky enthusiast, for buying, drinking and supporting their products – and for buying this book!

At a personal level, I'd like to thank the long-suffering but ever patient Mrs Buxton for mopping my increasingly fevered brow during the production of yet another book.

The team of Judy Moir (agent); Jonathan Taylor (publisher); Emma Tait (editor) and Lynn Carr (designer) have done a great job – grateful and fulsome thanks to all of them. And to Patrick Insole for another creative variation on the 101 theme for the jacket design. Together they have helped more than they know.

Finally, please support the growing craft-distilling industry with your credit cards! Especially now, new small businesses need your money.

Artisanal distilling at Abhainn Dearg, Isle of Lewis, Scotland.

Locally designed and built stills at La Alazana, Las Golondrinas, Chubut, Argentina.